VIALS OF WISDOM FOR THE WINNING WOMAN

Short Inspirational Reads Packed with Wisdom

Nicola Maxwell-Johnson

Author: Nicola Maxwell-Johnson

Printed in the United States of America.
First Edition, 2025.

ISBN: 979-8-218-88842-8

For permissions, inquiries, or speaking engagements, contact:
womenofpowerimprovingnicely@gmail.com or
nicolamaxwelljohnson@gmail.com

Dedication

To my mother, Desrine Douse - your unwavering resilience and tireless efforts, hard work, and sacrifice have shaped my life in profound ways. Even in the most adverse situations, you have demonstrated remarkable strength and grit.

To my husband, Michael, and our children, Joelle and Judah - you give my life immeasurable value and meaning. I love you dearly.

To my siblings, nieces, and nephews - my heart is full of gratitude for each of you. I thank God continually for blessing my life with your presence.

To every woman who, despite challenges and obstacles, keeps pushing forward and refuses to give up because she knows it is the intention of our Heavenly Father that we WIN - I salute you. May this book remind you that victory is already written in your story.

In Loving Memory

Of my beloved brother

Larmarr A. Lawes

(July 11, 1988 – November 21, 2022)

Your memory continues to live in the deepest corners of my heart. You were the epitome of kindness and bravery, and your light remains with me always.

Epigraph

"Nay, in all these things we are more than conquerors through Him that loved us."
Rom. 8:37 (KJV)

"Beloved, I wish above all things that thou mayest prosper and be in health, even as thy soul prospereth."
3 John 1:2 (KJV)

"I had fainted, unless I had believed to see the goodness of the Lord in the land of the living."
Psa. 27:13 (KJV)

Foreword

Compact into this book are 50 vials of wisdom that inspire you quickly to action, stir you to become a better version of yourself, and elevate you to heights unimaginable in the Lord Jesus Christ.

For those who are intentional about discovering how to navigate through the vicissitudes of life with resilience and adaptability, this is a must-read.

The Vials of Wisdom – written essentially for women to break the glass ceilings with practical advice, and real-life examples - are geared at stimulating the body, soul, and mind of its reader to a posture of great success and endless possibilities.

The treasure to be garnered within each vial presents a rich tapestry of motivational discourses coupled with contemporary ideas that will catapult women from all strata of society to become catalytic agents of change.

 The brevity of each segment provides great ease for reading and time to reflect and make application to lead a godly and action-packed life.

"There is no single defined path that we all must take in order to get to our intended destinations," posits the author of this book. Therefore, let us make good the path set before us, as we apply the wisdom encapsulated in this book to our advantage.

The Vials of Wisdom will definitely serve its audience faithfully, as a well-thought-out and readily available "roadmap for tenacious women on a journey to win."

Dr. Jasmin A. Rose

Preface

VIALS OF WISDOM FOR THE WINNING WOMAN was birthed from real experiences, deep reflection, prayer, and the deep conviction that God has woven purpose, strength, and victory into the very fabric of every woman's life. For years, I have carried the desire to encourage, uplift, and empower women - women who face battles silently, who hold families together, who push through heartache, who love deeply, and who rise, even when their wings feel worn.

This book is not written from a place of perfection, but from a place of process. It is shaped by lessons learned in valley seasons and victories won on mountaintops. Every vial is infused with insight drawn from moments where God revealed truth, hope, and healing into my heart.

My prayer is that as you journey through these pages, you will feel seen, strengthened, and reminded of who you are in Christ. You are chosen. You are loved. You are purposeful, and you are DESTINED TO WIN.

May these "Vials" of wisdom refresh your soul, ignite your faith, and embolden you to walk in divine confidence, knowing that the God who started His good work in you will surely complete it.

Acknowledgements

I am deeply grateful to God, the Author and Finisher of my faith, for His unwavering presence, His guiding hand, and His perfect wisdom. Every word in this book is a testament to His grace, His patience, and His love toward me. Without Him, none of this would be possible.

To my husband, Michael, and our children, Joelle and Judah, you are my daily blessings. Thank you for your love, patience, and understanding throughout this writing journey. Your support has been a steady anchor, and your presence fills my life with meaning.

To my church family, friends, and mentors who have prayed for me, believed in me, and offered words of wisdom when I needed them most, thank you for being pillars of strength and support. Your faith in me helped bring this book to life. To every spiritual leader who has spoken life into me and has been obedient to God and has released a prophetic word to me, it is because of you that this book became a reality.

To my friend Terryann, thank you for offering your expertise when I called upon you. I am forever grateful for your invaluable input and constructive feedback. May you forever be blessed!

To my Nigerian editor Praise, thank you for your expertise. Your attention to details and dedication to this project is highly appreciated. Your finishing touches certainly completed this book. I pray for continued blessings in your life and business.

To every woman who has shared her story, her struggle, her triumph, or even a simple moment of vulnerability with me, you have inspired these pages. Your courage and resilience remind me daily why this message is necessary.

And finally, to you, the reader, thank you for allowing me into your heart and your journey. My prayer is that these words uplift you, strengthen you, and remind you of the victorious, purposeful, God-ordained woman you are.

With love and gratitude,
Nicola

Introduction

ife has a way of stretching us. It demands courage, resilience, and hope even in moments when we feel empty. As women, we balance responsibilities, nurture others, carry silent burdens, and often show strength in seasons that attempt to break us. Yet through it all, God calls us *more than conquerors - He wants us to WIN*. He reminds us that His plans for us are good, that His love for us is unfailing, and that right here in the land of the living, we will see His goodness.

This book was written with you in mind, the woman who is determined to rise, who refuses to quit, and who knows deep down that WINNING is her God-ordained destiny. Whether you are navigating trials, waiting on God, rebuilding your confidence, or stepping boldly into purpose, these vials are designed to speak life into your spirit.

Within these pages, you will find encouragement, Biblical wisdom, personal reflections, and practical insights inspired by real stories, intimate encounters with God, and lessons gathered along my own journey. Think of each vial as a gentle reminder that you are not alone. God is for you. His Word is your compass. His strength is your advantage. His love is your anchor.

As you read, may you be empowered to let go of what no longer serves you, embrace who God says you are, and step fully into the victorious life He intended for you.

You are a WINNING WOMAN, and it's time to flourish and morph into the better version of yourself.

Scripture Version Note

Throughout this book, multiple Bible translations are used to bring clarity, depth, and richness to each vial. These include, but are not limited to:

- King James Version (KJV)

- New International Version (NIV)

- New Living Translation (NLT)

- English Standard Version (ESV)

- New King James Version (NKJV)

All Scripture quotations are referenced with their respective translation. Where no version is indicated, the KJV is used by default. Readers are encouraged to reflect on these scriptures in the translation that brings them the greatest personal understanding and spiritual insight.

Direct scriptures are in bold throughout the book.

Table of Contents

Section 1:

THE HEART OF A WINNING WOMAN & SPIRITUAL MATURITY.

Identity, Mindset, Foundational Strength, Emotional Courage.

"Above all else, guard your heart, for everything you do flows from it."

(Prov. 4:23)

❖───────◆◆───────❖

Every winning woman begins her journey from the inside out. Her victory is not birthed from circumstances but from the strength, resilience, and faith that dwell deep within her heart.

In this section of the book, you will find vials that invite you to nurture the inner woman: her emotions, her identity, her hope, and her courage.

As you read these vials and meditate on the accompanying scriptures, may you rediscover the truth that you are equipped, empowered, and embraced by God. You carry within you a strength that adversity cannot break and a light that darkness cannot extinguish.

Flush It With LOVE

I once encountered a sagacious woman whose words of wisdom have outlived her. One of her favorite maxims that still resonates with me is. "Flush it with LOVE!" By this, she simply meant: " GET OVER IT! LET IT GO!

Now, when we excrete waste, we are all happy to quickly flush it away, right? It is with the same urgency that we should aspire to get rid of things that cause us distress - FLUSH IT WITH LOVE!

If something/someone disturbs your peace - FLUSH IT WITH LOVE!

Do you feel that you were treated unfairly? - FLUSH IT WITH LOVE!

Someone offended you, maybe even lied on you? - FLUSH IT WITH LOVE!

Were you betrayed? - FLUSH IT WITH LOVE!

I guess you get the picture by now...just FLUSH IT WITH LOVE!

As you read, you may think, 'Easier said than done!' Certainly, as humans, our first response may be to strike back, to curse, to seek revenge, or any other action that we may deem fitting for the wrong that has been meted out to us. These reactions may give us feelings of gratification even for a moment. The score is settled! There! We're even now! But think for a moment -be honest- how much of a solution do these reactions guarantee? After all is said and done, we may still be bitter, resentful, or any other negative emotion.

What do I do then? FLUSH IT WITH LOVE! FORGIVE! LET IT GO! LEAVE IT IN GOD'S HANDS! This doesn't mean that you are a fool. It simply means that you value your inner peace, and you know that you are not responsible for the actions (or inactions) of others. Also, it's you saying, "I'll just leave this to God". Others may even say Karma.

Numerous scriptures tell us to just relax, let some things be, just forgive!

➢ 2 Chron. 20:15b - **For the battle is not yours, but God's.**

➢ Rom. 12: 19 - **Beloved, do not avenge yourselves, but rather give place to wrath; for it is written, "Vengeance is Mine, I will repay," says the Lord.**

➢ Prov. 15: 1 - **A soft answer turneth away wrath: but grievous words stir up anger.**

➢ Eph. 4: 31 - 32 - **Let all bitterness, and wrath, and anger, and clamour, and evil speaking, be put away from you, with all malice: And be ye kind one to another, tenderhearted, forgiving one another, even as God for Christ's sake hath forgiven you.**

> Matt. 6: 14 - 15 - **For if ye forgive men their trespasses, your heavenly Father will also forgive you: But if ye forgive not men their trespasses, neither will your Father forgive your trespasses.**

So, next time you are wronged and feel like being belligerent, meditate on these scriptures and just ... FLUSH IT WITH LOVE!

Apologizing is Free and Freeing

There is usually a lot of talk about forgiveness and healing; however, we do not hear the same amount of chatter urging folks to APOLOGIZE. We may dwell on talking about forgiveness simply because we feel as though it removes our responsibility to apologize. Here's the truth, though: if we should apologize to someone and don't, even if we are forgiven, that apology is still owed. Yes, we may hear things such as "forgiveness has nothing to do with the offender but rather the offended" and "it is your responsibility to forgive". While these statements may ring true, apologizing is just as critical. In fact, many see apologizing as admitting guilt and refuse to do so because of pride.

Matt. 5:23-24 teaches us that if you are offering your gift at the altar and remember that your brother or sister has something against you, 24 leave your gift there in front of the altar. First go and be reconciled to them; then come and offer your gift. This scripture is often interpreted from the viewpoint that it is the other person who has done you wrong, and the reconciliation that is done is forgiveness. I wish, however, to challenge this viewpoint and propose that this scripture is actually instructing us to go and APOLOGIZE to the 'brother or sister' whom we have wronged. Think about it this way: the individual has something against you, not out of malice or envy, but because you have hurt them and owe them an APOLOGY.

So, before we run off with our tails in our backs to offer our sacrifice to God- you know, doing all the church and Christian things that we do, pause and introspect: who has an ought against you? What is the real reason for this ought? Is it because they are harboring malice and hatred towards you, or is it because you have wronged them? - knowingly or unknowingly. Our ego and pride might be screaming, "You have nothing to apologize for!" Apologize even if you were in the right. Apologize, especially if you are wrong, because not doing so is immature, selfish, and 'un-christlike'. Live in peace with all men (Heb 12:14) and to do so may very well require that we APOLOGIZE. Finally, Owe no man anything (Rom. 13:8) - not even an apology.

Freedom in Forgiveness

Then Peter came to him and asked, "Lord, how often should I forgive someone who sins against me? Seven times?" "No, not seven times," Jesus replied, "but seventy times seven! This scripture from Matthew 18: 21-22 is usually quoted whenever the topic of forgiveness is brought up. Immediately after the parable of The Unmerciful Servant is told (Matt. 18: 23 - 34). Jesus concluded this lesson on forgiveness with these words: "This is how my heavenly Father will treat each of you unless you forgive your brother or sister from your heart." (Matt. 18:35).

Believe me, I know, FORGIVENESS CAN BE DIFFICULT! Hurt can be so hard to process and to overcome. We might have experienced traumatic situations that crushed our spirits. Some people have even been physically harmed by others. And are we expected to forgive? Quite a preposterous expectation, some might say. Nonetheless, as Jesus taught, forgiveness is a must.

You may ask, how can I forgive someone who has done wrong to me? I was innocent! I did nothing wrong! I was faithful and loyal! True, even all those reasonings still do not relieve us of our responsibility to forgive. The moment we start to view forgiveness as a personal necessity and responsibility, the concept might become easier to grasp. If we should turn the search light inward and honestly reflect on the many times that we have done wrong and our loving Heavenly

Father, in His tender mercies, has seen it fitting to forgive us, then we would begin to realize, too, that those who have done us wrong are deserving of forgiveness.

Sometimes we struggle with forgiving others because we believe that this will absolve the person of whatever appropriate punishment they should receive for having hurt us. Not so. The onus is on us. Think of it this way, forgiveness is our duty, whilst vengeance is the Lord's doing. (Rom 12:19; Deut. 32:35)

Can we forget some of the horrible things that others have done to us? Probably not, but can we forgive? Yes, it's in our power to do so. While it may be a difficult task to forgive, it is within our power to do so. Therefore, forgive and let God do the rest.

Don't be ashamed of your shame! Be empowered by it.

Life sometimes throws us some unexpected curveballs. We falter, we stumble, we fall. Some of us carry shame from the past. There might have been things in our lives that we are not proud of; skeletons in the closet that we pray are never revealed. So, we become ashamed of our shame, and the devil might very well use our shame from the past to taunt us, causing us to cower in fear and hang our heads low in shame.

Hope can be found in 2 Cor. 5:17 that declares "Therefore if any man be in Christ, he is a new creature: old things are passed away; behold, all things have become new." A life in Christ signifies newness, a fresh start. Christ wipes our slate clean and drops all charges. Hallelujah! Therefore, no longer be ashamed of your shame. By no means should we flaunt and brag about our shame simply because the charges have been dropped. Instead, we should embrace the new beginnings, learn the lessons from the past, and use them as launching pads as we evolve from day to day.

The truth is that our shame can teach us some valuable lessons that we can, in turn, utilize to help others who are facing similar situations and are feeling a sense of hopelessness. Having gained firsthand experience with some challenging life situations fully qualifies us to help someone walk through their period of turmoil. Coming out on the other side of our shame is excellent proof to everyone that redemption and restoration are not just fiction but realities.

The shame that was meant to stain and tarnish our reputations and destroy our destiny can instead be turned into beautiful canvases that exude the great power of the Almighty God. What was meant to keep us bound in the throes of disgrace can become beautiful stories of conquering the odds that were meant to eradicate us. Certainly, the pain, bitterness, and anger from our shameful circumstances might still be lingering in our lives, but they are no match for the liberating power of our God. The days of shame are behind you; it is now time to rise from the ashes and go forth with the peace and blessings of the Lord. Remember, he gives beauty for ashes (Isaiah 61:3). You are beautiful!

Unearthing the Winner in You

Being a woman is truly unique. We are created differently: biologically, emotionally, and spiritually. We wear multiple hats and carry multiple identities. We are mothers, wives, bosses, friends, sisters, daughters, pastors, leaders, caregivers, and so much more. Life does not always give us the luxury of choosing just one role at a time. Instead, we often find ourselves juggling all of them simultaneously. This constant balancing act can leave us tired, overworked, and completely worn out. Added to this, society often places stereotypes and limitations on women, which can further deepen our feelings of inadequacy or invisibility.

But here is the undeniable truth: there is a WINNER in every woman. Sadly, not every woman sees this truth immediately. Some never recognize the strength and brilliance that lie within, while others discover it but fear allowing that indomitable spirit to rise to the surface. Yet God makes it absolutely clear that we were BORN TO WIN.

Romans 8:37 declares that we are *"**more than conquerors**."* This alone is proof that God intends for us to walk in victory. Not only does He want us to win, but He has already equipped us with every resource we need. 2 Peter 1:3 (AMP) reminds us that: **"His divine**

power has bestowed on us [absolutely] everything necessary for [a dynamic spiritual] life and godliness…."

Still, the reality is that we do not always *feel* victorious. We do not always feel strong, capable, or prepared to conquer anything. And yet, the call remains: Unearth the WINNER in You!

So why are so many women not living victorious lives? Could it be that the Winner within has been lying dormant? Perhaps she is buried under layers of pain, disappointment, fear, trauma, or exhaustion. Whatever the cause, the Winner must be awakened, nurtured, and activated.

There is a profound difference between being *planted* and being *buried*. A simple way to determine which one applies to you is to examine whether growth is occurring. If nothing is growing: no progress, no fruit, no movement, then perhaps you have been buried beneath the weight of life's pressures. And like a priceless treasure hidden in the earth, you must be unearthed. Just as Lazarus lay in the tomb until Jesus called him forth, the Winner inside of you is waiting for a divine summons: "Come forth… arise… emerge… be activated."

For too long, many women have believed the enemy's lies:
"You are good for nothing."
"You are not enough."
"You will never succeed."

"You will not recover from this."

"You weren't meant for greatness."

Others have shrunken back in fear, embraced doubt, or settled into the false belief that a mediocre life is all they deserve. The burdens of life have weakened some women to the point of hopelessness, draining them of their courage and will to continue.

But hear this: **You were NOT created for mediocrity.**
Jesus declared, *"I have come that they may have life, and have it in abundance."* (John 10:10) Personalize this scripture by inserting your name into that promise!

Since Christ has called you to an abundant, thriving, victorious life, you cannot afford to let the Winner inside you remain dormant. She must awaken to purpose and action. God has deposited unique gifts, talents, and strengths in you: not only for your benefit, but to bless and uplift others.

For this reason, and for your destiny:
It is time to UNEARTH THE WINNER IN YOU.

YOU CAN DO IT!

A simple truth is that life comes with no manual; there is no blueprint. There is no one way in which we should go about things. There is no single defined path that we all must take in order to get to our intended destinations. Life is as beautiful as it is ugly, as easy as it is challenging, as simple as it is complicated. No two people have the exact journey from birth to death. Yes, there may be some commonalities, but in the end, we will all chart different courses.

Whilst we can lend a helping hand, give a listening ear, offer words of wisdom, or simply observe from the sidelines, in the end, we can do so much and no more for others (or others for us). There comes that time when we will either have to 'woman-up' and face life or resort to the alternative of shying away from the good, the bad, and the ugly that life brings and just merely 'exist'.

We were never created to merely exist; there is an abundance of life to enjoy! Joh. 10:10b states **"I am come that they may have life, and that they might have it more abundantly"**. Jesus came that we may have an abundant life! What a glorious thing! We all have a mandate to accomplish! Yes, there is purpose in each of us, and we are divinely equipped with all that we need to fulfil this mandate. 2 Pet. 1:3 reminds us that **"According as his divine power hath given unto us**

all things that pertain unto life and godliness, through the knowledge of him that hath called us to glory and virtue."

While fulfilling our Godly purpose may be challenging, it is indeed possible. And life can be fulfilling! And the beauty about it is that YOU CAN DO IT!! For sure, there will be disappointments, heartaches, frustration, and pain, but these come only to make the journey a more colourful one. Despite the odds that you may encounter, YOU CAN DO IT!!

Some time ago, I came across an article about a man who wanted to sue his parents for giving birth to him. The essence of the story was that the young man felt that his parents should have sought his permission before giving birth to him. Quite befuddling! This young man based his argument on the notion known as Anti-Natalism. Anti-natalism is an ideology that argues that life is so full of misery that people should stop procreating immediately. People who are of this philosophical opinion are of the view that there is no point to humanity, and as such, if humans were to become extinct, then Earth and animals would be much better off. People who embrace this belief think that human suffering is enough reason why humanity should not exist.

It is disheartening to realize that some people hold such views. Let's all face it; life can be challenging! We were given no guide as to how to maneuver through the labyrinth of this mystery called LIFE. However, with Jesus as the Captain of our ship, we can live a fulfilling, purposeful, and joyous life. It is the will of God that the Earth be populated with HUMANS! After all, he instructed Adam in Ge. 1:28 to **"Be fruitful, and multiply, and replenish the earth"**. Any viewpoint to the contrary is not only erroneous but also ungodly.

Thus far, my life has been a rather colorful journey. It has been filled with ups and downs, ins and outs, highs and lows, tears and laughter. Through it all, however, it has all been worth it. In retrospect, there is not much (if anything) that I would change because each of my experiences and challenges has helped to shape me into the individual that I have become.

There was a period, particularly in my childhood years, when I questioned the reason for my existence. I would spend hours thinking: Where did I come from? Why am I here? Wouldn't it be better if I just did not exist? No one really wanted me around! In such a vast world, you are nothing but insignificant! I struggled with these thoughts for a number of years. No one really knew that such thoughts occupied the forefront of my mind. For years, I would endure these mental torments. They got more intense as my struggles became harder. The thoughts tormented me more as the weight of my burdens grew heavier. Certainly, there were times when I wished (even prayed a little) that I could just disappear to a place where everything would be just wonderful. To a place where I would feel loved and simply happy. I mean a literal place in the here-and-now. Not a place in the grave!

If I could just be rich, the…! If I had parents who were…! If I were from a country that…! If I were from a family that…! In my view, all these IFs would just make everything fine! Somehow, through this period, I never had thoughts of stopping. There was this FORCE within me that kept urging me to go on, and I am happy and grateful that God was (and has always been) with me, guiding me along each winding path and protecting me as I traverse treacherous paths. So, no matter what life throws at you – get up, brush yourself off, consult God, and keep moving on. Never lose sight of the fact that you matter and are here in the land of the living for a purpose. By the grace of God – YOU CAN DO IT! Whatever 'IT' means to you!

BE BLESSED!

Living the Winning Life

LIVING THE WINNING LIFE speaks to the fact that God wants us to flourish even amidst difficult circumstances. It's a mode of living and a way of doing. Declaring that you are LIVING THE WINNING LIFE is an act of faith and even a prophetic declaration. It is you declaring your unshakeable confidence in the Heavenly Father, knowing His capabilities and trusting firmly in His goodness towards you. It is also coming to an understanding that you carry within you the spirit of excellence that you have been endowed with by the Almighty. It's knowing that you are favored and divinely blessed.

LIVING THE WINNING LIFE is knowing and fully embracing that you carry the blessings of Deuteronomy 28: 1-13. 1 Peter 2: 9 informs us that **"you are a chosen people, a royal priesthood, a holy nation, God's special possession, that you may declare the praises of him who called you out of darkness into his wonderful light."** The evidence is clear! We are WINNERS!

Do not believe, though, that living a winning life exempts us from life's challenges and struggles. It does not. In fact, the Winning Life can look like patience and endurance through difficult seasons and handling life's challenges with grace and divine wisdom. However, as a winner, we begin to face and respond to challenges differently.

We have an optimistic outlook on life. We look for the 'good in all things' (Rom. 8:28). We believe God's Word above what the physical realities tell us (Heb. 11:1).

Winning looks different for everyone. It does not mean that you are always at the front or ahead of everyone else. No, the Winning Life is not about speed or an ordinal position. Living the Winning Life isn't about competing with others. It is a life of intentionality and focus. It is discovering your life's purpose and walking boldly in it: unafraid and unashamed. It is collaborating with other winners for the greater good. It is supporting others with your expertise and resources. It is being kind to yourself and others.

A life of salvation, obedience, and surrender to Christ is a WINNING LIFE.

Time to Reflect

SECTION I: THE HEART OF A WINNING WOMAN & SPIRITUAL MATURITY

Identity • Inner Healing • Emotional Courage • Spiritual Maturity

1. Flush It With LOVE

1. What emotions or thoughts am I still holding onto that God is inviting me to release?

2. How can I choose to love today, even in situations that feel difficult or unfair?

3. Who (or what) do I need to forgive to experience deeper peace?

2. Apologizing is Free and Freeing

1. Is pride or fear preventing me from apologizing where I should?

2. How does a sincere apology make space for healing: both for me and the other person?

3. What relationships could be strengthened by humility and openness?

---

3. Freedom in Forgiveness

1. What burden am I still carrying that forgiveness can release?

2. How can I reflect Christ's forgiveness more intentionally in my daily life?

3. What does "freedom" look like for me right now?

---

4. Don't Be Ashamed of Your Shame! Be Empowered by It

1. What areas of my life have I allowed shame to silence or limit me?

2. How can I turn my past pain into purpose?

3. What truth from God's Word can replace the lies shame has spoken over me?

5. Unearthing the Winner in You

1. What qualities has God already placed in me that I sometimes overlook?

2. What limiting beliefs are standing in the way of my potential?

3. What would my life look like if I fully embraced the "winner" God created me to be?

6. YOU CAN DO IT!

1. What step is God asking me to take that requires courage right now?

2. What would I attempt if I truly believed that God is with me?

3. How can I strengthen my faith and confidence today?

7. Living the Winning Life

1. What does a "winning life" mean to me in a spiritual sense?

2. Which habits, thoughts, or relationships help me grow—and which hinder me?

3. What is one practical change I can make this week to align my life with God's purpose?

Section 11:

RELATIONSHIPS, LOVE, & COMMUNITY.

Friendships, God's Love,

Relational Wisdom, Connection.

"Let all that you do be done in love."

(1 Cor. 16:14)

We were never designed to do life alone. Relationships, whether friendships, family, or spiritual connections, are vital to our growth and purpose.

This section explores the beauty of godly relationships, the gift of solitude, and the constancy of God's love.

As you read, may you discover how to nurture meaningful connections while honoring your own space, boundaries, and emotional well-being.

Who are your friends?

There is a fascinating story in Lk. 5:17-39 and Mk 2:3-11, where a paralyzed man was brought to Jesus by four of his friends. The friends didn't just take him to Jesus to be healed. They went through great struggles to get him there. Scriptures don't record the distance that they carried him, but it does detail that in order to get to Jesus, they had to remove a section of the roof in order to let him down into the room to Jesus. Imagine how challenging that entire operation was and the strength and determination that the friends exhibited. Remember too that this was not a personal mission! No, they all collaborated on behalf of their friend. This act was absolutely amazing!

Think about your own friends - how supportive are they? Would they do such an act for you? Would you do this for them? It is very important to have friends - not just any friends, good friends. Friendship should be mutually beneficial and not one-sided. The right friends add value to our lives. They inspire, support, motivate, and encourage. Our friends should also challenge us to do better and be able to correct us in love and tell us the truth- even if it is difficult for us to hear.

Our friends should be there in all seasons of your life - during the good and the bad. Different individuals will have unique strengths and perspectives that they bring to friendships. Friendships should be pure and selfless (but not self-sacrificing). True friends are understanding and mindful of each other's boundaries. Being friends does not give us the right to invade personal space and privacy.

We should be able to discern when our friends need us to 'step up' or to 'stand down'. Some situations require our presence and actions, while others call for our presence and prayers. Friends see needs and voids in each other's lives and do what they can to assist. It is not mentioned whether it was the paralyzed man who asked to be taken to Jesus or his friends who offered - and it doesn't matter. What's important is that the paralyzed friend was brought to Jesus and was healed. Do you have a friend whom you might need to "carry to Jesus"?

Embrace Friendships, But Cherish the Gift of Solitude.

"No man is an island; no man stands alone" are words that were penned by the 17th-century poet John Donne. These words allude to the obvious interconnectedness of humanity. The words carry great significance and have been echoed throughout the ages. For sure, we all need other humans. As independent as we may want to claim that we are, we definitely need others. If we are to thrive in life, we need a community. We need people. We need friends.

Now, what's certain is that we are not for everyone, and everyone is not for us. Do you know someone with whom you don't get along well for whatever reason? Maybe there isn't even any animosity; you just don't click. Yet, this person gets along well with many others; perhaps even with others with whom you get along well. The point is, we will never be friends with everyone, but that does not negate the fact that we need friends.

Genuine friends are blessings from God. They are there to help guide us through life's tough seasons. They are there to walk with us through our dark days, to laugh with us when times are good, and to dry our tears when times get challenging. Friends are there to offer assistance and to cheer us on. They are there to correct us and to steer us back on the right path when we veer off track. Friends are valuable, and we need at least a few good ones in our lives.

A word of caution, though - be vigilant with friendships. Whilst friends are blessings, be careful so as not to miss the value of solitude. Sometimes we can become so absorbed and engrossed in friendships that we begin to lose ourselves in the mix. Solitude, just like friendships, has great benefits. Thus, we need to embrace and value it. Solitude does not mean isolation nor neglecting human contact altogether. Instead, it means finding value and even pleasure in being alone.

Spending time alone gives us the opportunity to better understand who we are. We get time to rest and decompress, to introspect, to develop creativity, among many other things. Some folks are so used to being with others and being enthralled by their company that they secretly fear being by themselves. However, instead of fearing being alone, solitude should be viewed as a cherished gift.

Yes, develop and maintain great friendships. Do not simply seek out great friendships but also be a great friend. Do not forget to value and embrace time alone. At suitable intervals, be sure to spend time with yourself. Reflect, relax, and renew body, mind, and soul. Not only does spending time in solitude benefit you, but it's also beneficial to your friends since it makes you a better person and, in turn, a better friend.

God's Love Is Constant!

Lam 3: 22-23 declares, "**The steadfast love of the Lord never ceases; his mercies never come to an end; they are new every morning; great is your faithfulness.** This is the truth! God's love and goodness are constant. They are ever-present and not conditional. There is a line in the well-known song by Jireh by Elevation Worship and Maverick City Music that says, "I'll never be more loved than I am right now". At first, I didn't pay much attention to the depth of the meaning of that line until one day it really dawned on me and just how true those words are! God already loves us to the MAXIMUM! His love and goodness are pure and shall forever be with us. His goodness towards us is not contingent on how perfect we are. Don't get me wrong now - He definitely expects us to obey His word, live by His ordinances, and to fully embrace His will for our lives.

Nonetheless, when we 'mess up' and do wrong, He still loves us. So do not let our mistakes or shortcomings guilt us into feeling as though we are not worthy of God's love. Again, I remind you that you are already loved to the maximum. Psa. 23:6 declare - **Surely goodness and mercy shall follow me all the days of my life.** Note - all the days of my life, not just some days. And along with goodness, there is the companion - mercy. That is simply God refraining from punishing us for our wrongs. My friend, you are loved. I wish that there was another way to fully express this to you, but simply put, God loves you! In spite of your mess.

Yes, you might have disappointed Him, faltered along the way, but take comfort in the fact that God's love is with you every day. We serve a perfect God who does not hold grudges nor keep scores. Oh, how liberating that is! You see, sometimes we tend to view God, considering how we view other humans. But remember - we cannot in any way, shape, or form begin to fathom how great God is. He's beyond our scope to figure out. So do not try to figure out how He could still love someone like you. Just accept it! Embrace it! Be liberated by it! Know that God's love for you, yes, you, is constant!

Time to Reflect

SECTION II: RELATIONSHIPS, LOVE & COMMUNITY

Friendships • Love • Boundaries • Connection • Support Systems

---

1. Who Are Your Friends?

1. Who are the three people I can trust with my heart and spiritual journey?

2. What qualities make someone a true friend to me?

3. Are there friendships I've outgrown but have struggled to release?

4. How can I be a better friend: more present, supportive, or prayerful?

---

2. Embrace Friendships, But Cherish the Gift of Solitude

1. Do I find it easy or difficult to be alone with myself? Why?

2. What emotions arise when I am in solitude (peace, fear, anxiety, clarity)?

3. How can solitude become a space of healing and restoration?

4. What boundaries do I need in order to protect my alone time without feeling guilty?

---

3. God's Love Is Constant!

1. How has God shown His love to me in ways I may have overlooked?

2. What lies do I sometimes believe about God's love?

3. How can I allow God's love to heal areas where human love has disappointed me?

4. What changes when I choose to see myself the way God sees me?

💛 BONUS: Deep-Heart Reflection

Ask yourself:

- Who am I when I'm truly loved, and who am I when I feel unloved?

- How has God used relationships to grow me?

- What does God want to teach me about love in this season and beyond?

- Which relationships do I need to forgive, redefine, or strengthen?

Section III:

EMOTIONAL & MENTAL

WELL-BEING.

Thought life, Emotional Regulation, Inner Battles, Mental Clarity.

"You will keep him in perfect peace whose mind is stayed on You."

(Isa. 26:3)

Our minds and emotions are powerful, yet they are also vulnerable spaces. A Winning Woman learns to care for her internal world with grace, wisdom, and intentionality.

This section centers on quieting anxious thoughts, embracing imperfections, releasing burdens, and finding balance.

As you reflect on these vials, may you experience renewed peace and clarity. God desires wholeness for you - emotionally, mentally, and spiritually.

The Dangers of Overthinking!

Yes! Read the title again! Overthinking is dangerous! We may all be aware of this truth, but that does not stop us from engaging in this very dangerous practice. The mind is a very powerful thing that can control us if we allow it to. It may be a bit of a complex concept to fully understand, but, in essence, we should control our minds and not the other way around. An uncontrolled mind can be like a loaded gun left in the hands of the wrong person. It will cause devastation and utter chaos! 2 Cor. 10:5 admonishes us to "**Cast[ing] down imaginations, and every high thing that exalteth itself against the knowledge of God and bring[ing] into captivity every thought to the obedience of Christ.** See, we have to take authority over our thoughts and not yield to the temptation to overthink, because often, what our minds lead us to think is not the truth! Our minds are battlefields that the enemy targets, and one of the strategies is the act of overthinking. Do not let the enemy gain access and dominion over your mind! Protect your mind; guard it from the invasions of the devil!

Have you ever been lied to or at least thought that you were being lied to? We sit and observe the actions of others and how they react to us or treat us, and instantaneously, we start to put the pieces together. Well, this doesn't make sense. He/She said this or did that. It's just not adding up! Sounds familiar? How often do you go on such a rampage? When was the last time that your mind has led you down a long, winding path of psychoanalyzing what your spouse, family, coworker, or friends did or said? I am sure you feel convinced that you know just what the person really meant by what they did/said. Again, even when we feel as though we know it all because we have sat and figured it out and put the pieces of the puzzle together, we could still be very wrong. So, do yourself a favor and stop overthinking! It does not help. Instead, this habit robs you of your peace, adds undue pressure on you, causes you to stress, and simply makes you unhappy.

I have always told myself that even when you don't go looking for it, you will eventually discover the truth. It's as if the truth will come knocking when you least expect it. You know what, if someone lies to you or willfully withholds the whole story, it is on them and not you! Don't get me wrong, I am by no means saying that we should simply allow people to get away with being deceptive! I totally believe in calling out people when we see the red flags and the holes in their stories. It is when they maintain their story that we should stop and leave them to their own devices. Do not get worked up and run to your corner and instantly begin to overthink.

Pray instead that God will reveal the truth, the whole truth, and nothing but the truth. Ask that God will reveal the hearts and intentions of those around you. Ask God for clarity and that every cover of deception and camouflage be lifted so that the truth can shine through. Ask for peace as you endure your storms and shift your focus to those things and people that bring you joy and peace. It's not that you should simply forget about the unsettling situation; you should instead lay it carefully in the hands of the Lord and allow Him to unravel it in His timing. Also, give people time to introspect and a chance to do the right thing because the truth is, there is nothing that your overthinking can do or change. The next time that you are tempted to overthink, do what Paul advises in Mt. 4:8 **whatsoever things are true, whatsoever things are honest, whatsoever things are just, whatsoever things are pure, whatsoever things are lovely, whatsoever things are of good report; if there be any virtue, and if there be any praise, think on these things.** Do it for your own peace of mind because God's got you!

Dealing with Mental Overload

Dozens of emails to sift through and reply to! Phone calls and text messages from everyone! Work assignments and deadlines to meet! Perhaps even school assignments, too! Did I pay this bill? When is that bill due? When is my child's next appointment? When is my next appointment? Ahhm, did I unplug the iron before I left home? Oh no, I forgot to take my medication AGAIN! When will the wedding/party that I got invited to be held? Hold on, but I haven't seen that pair of shoes for a while now! I wonder where it could be. Is that meeting/teacher conference today or tomorrow? Oh, I need a break, let me scroll through social media a bit! Let me see what this news item has to say, really quick. I promised my friend that I would call! Oops, it has been over 2 weeks, but I still haven't!

Does any of this sound familiar? It is the reality of so many of us. Mental overload can cause us to be physically exhausted without doing any great manual labor. It's like carrying a ton of bricks in our minds. It can be overwhelming at times. Sometimes there are so many demands on us that it wears us out. We can be stretched and stressed by it all. In short, it can be all too overwhelming and causes us to feel emotionally and physically worn. We could all use some more hours in our day, right? Or is it that we need less on our plate? Could it be that there's a need for better organization and 'time management'? Definitely, this is a lot to ponder on.

In the chaotic and fast-paced world that we live in, which can be filled with mayhem, it is very important for us to be very mindful of who we are and carefully categorize what's important from what's not. Imagine children playing with bubbles outside, and they decide to chase them all. The likely outcome is that they most definitely will NOT catch many. Similarly, it is important for us to prioritize and strategize so that we can find some amount of balance in order to avoid being burned out, stressed, overwhelmed, etc. What's important to get done? Is it a necessity? What's the timeline that you have to work with? Is it a must that you do it, or can the task be delegated to someone else?

I once heard someone say (or I might have read it somewhere): "You can't manage time-you manage yourself 'in time'". We hear talks about time management all the time, but the truth is - we cannot manipulate time. We will always only have so many hours in a day. The important thing is to be conscious of how we operate 'in time'. So, are we facing mental overload simply because we are not using time wisely? Are we procrastinating? Or is it a genuine case of just having too much to do?

Whatever the case may be, something must be done because self-preservation and optimal performance in all spheres of our lives are important. Take a step back, evaluate your situation, set a plan in motion, and work at it. If this plan does not work well, then keep revising your plan and devise a new one. Know when to hit the pause button! Do something fun that allows you to recharge and refresh yourself; regroup, then go again. Set boundaries and stick to them. Seek professional help if you need to. Most importantly, find some time to hide away in solace with God so that He can administer strength, grace, and divine wisdom that will fuel your very being. Just don't keep on going! Your fuse will burn out, and unfortunately, you may not get a chance to have it replaced or repaired.

Don't do it all alone! DELEGATE

There is a rather interesting story in Ex. 18:14 - 24 where Moses spent basically all day serving the people as a judge. Certainly, this was an important and necessary task. However, it was time-consuming and overwhelming for one person to undertake. Upon seeing what was taking place, Jethro - Moses' father-in-law gave him some valuable advice. In fact, Jethro chided Moses by telling him that "What you are doing is not good. You and these people who come to you will only wear yourselves out". While Moses had good intentions, he was biting off more than he could chew. Jethro introduced his son-in-law to DELEGATING.

You see, many of us are like Moses. In good faith, we tend to take on too many tasks that lead to burnout, not just of ourselves but also of others. Notice, Jethro mentioned that both Moses and the people who come to him will be worn out. What society has taught many of us is that "If we want something done well, then we must do it ourselves". And so, we find ourselves with an everlastingly long to-do list that leaves us worn out, stressed, agitated, and downright angry. We try to juggle things at home, work, church, among other places, and more often than not, this leaves us in a predicament - being physically exhausted, mentally drained, financially stretched, etc.

Jethro said to Moses, "The work is too heavy for you; you cannot handle it alone". Have you ever considered that this might be applicable to you? Delegating tasks is not a sign of weakness nor laziness! It is not passing on your responsibilities to others either! It's wisdom. It's self-preservation. It's sometimes the most viable option. When we delegate tasks to others, be it great or small, it is not an act that signifies that you are becoming resigned and willing to be replaced by others. Instead, it's a way of prioritizing things that are important as well as honing your skills.

Delegating is also an opportunity to identify and develop the skills of others around you. Moses was advised to find others to help him judge the people. This shows that there were others around him who were capable. These men got an opportunity to develop their skills while Moses got some 'ease'; his workload lightened, and the job was still being undertaken.

Therefore, think about what tasks you have that can be delegated to others. There may be simple tasks even within your household that you slavishly do that can be delegated to your children or other family members. Perhaps, there might even be someone in your department who may be better and more efficient at a task than you are, but you'll never know simply because you have failed to ask them. Certainly, there are some things that you and only you will or must do, but there are numerous other tasks that can be delegated. So, DON'T DO IT ALONE!

Be Mindful of Your Reactions

The scripture in Eph. 4:26a declares "**Be ye angry, and sin not**". My interpretation is that it is fine to be angry; however, we should be careful not to become so embroiled that we sin. Often, we encounter situations and circumstances that do cause us to become angry. Nonetheless, we must try to handle these situations as best as possible since, after it all blows over, we still need to have our integrity intact. The fact is that some people may willfully provoke individuals in order to get a negative reaction out of them.

The truth is that not everyone has our best interests at heart and might even be malicious in their intentions and their actions towards others. They will even know our 'buttons' and will purposely push them just so that they can provoke a negative reaction out of us. Picture a scenario where you are a puppet, and someone holds your control buttons, and they press them whenever they like. This is definitely not what we want for ourselves.

In the heat of the moment, when such a situation arises, it is less likely that we will remember not to get carried away and be pushed over the edge of anger into the realm of sinning. Hence, it would be good to give thought to this possibility from time to time so that when those moments do arise, we will be more in control of our emotions and actions.

Scripture implores us to be "**Be sober, be vigilant**" (1 Pet. 5:8a), and this applies to all areas of our lives. The adversary will seek every loophole to overthrow us, so we must stand fast in order to **resist the devil** (James. 4:7). Always be conscientious and do not allow people and situations to 'draw you out' (cause you to act out of character), for, in the end you are the one who will be left feeling remorseful and possibly in need of repentance. Remember, "**Be ye angry, and sin not**" (Eph 4:26a).

Emotions Are Fickle - Beware!

We are complex beings who have been fearfully and wonderfully made (Psa. 139:14). Our Creator intricately designed us and paid keen attention to our every detail (Luk. 12:7). He even wired us with emotions that help us to experience life in unique ways. Emotions are varied and manifest in pleasant forms such as joy and happiness. There are also the not-so-nice ones, for example: sadness, fear, and anger. Emotions are very temporary, and so we have to be very mindful of them - both the good and bad ones.

Our emotions can be easily triggered; consequently, we have to be watchful and not allow them to get the better of us. Prov. 4:23 cautions that you **guard your heart**. Perhaps, like me, you can think back to a time when you experienced a bout of emotions that you would have preferred not to have, but it was very difficult to 'shake' or to 'get over'. Our emotions might lead us to overthink and even become confused. Sometimes, the 'evidence' that we see around us and the emotions that we feel do not align, and this can place us into an even worse situation. We might even feel cornered and trapped by our negative emotions, and it's not like there is a switch that we can use to turn our emotions on or off as we would like. Hence, it is important to be aware of and monitor our emotions so that we do not end up on an emotional roller coaster.

If we are not careful, our emotions can lead us to say and do things that we might later regret. Therefore, we should never make decisions when we are very emotional, whether it is good or bad emotions. This is because emotions tend to cloud our judgement, and we might not be diligent enough to take all variables into consideration and, in the long run, end up regretting what we have said and done. Instead, ground decisions, thoughts, and actions in logic, truth, Godly wisdom, and discernment. Take a step back, allow some time to 'clear your head', pray, read God's word, and seek clarity and direction from the Lord. Trust in the LORD with all your heart; do not depend on your own understanding (Prov. 3:5). Our own understanding can be easily tampered with by our emotions - so it's best to trust in our All-Knowing God. Remember, feelings are fickle, so don't give them a chance to vote.

Embracing our imperfections

I got a new phone two days ago. YEAH ME! The truth is, I am not fussy about such things, but when I went to inquire about the costs, I realized that upgrading wasn't so bad after all, so I figured, "Why not?" Now, this phone is the latest! Top notch, I tell you! The camera quality is superior. So superior that I don't know if I will ever be comfortable enough to take a selfie again. "Why?" you may ask, because it shows every spot, every blemish, the bushy eyebrows, every 'ugly thing' in my face. Seriously, I could do well without that negativity right now. This camera is simply too good! To go further, I have a bit of time on my hands, and so my attention was drawn to my cuticles. To put it mildly, these fingers need HELP! And you know what? If I continue to inspect my body, I am going to come up with so many more imperfections. There's so much that I would want to be some other way, to be better, to be perfect.

Don't misunderstand me- I am a huge advocate for self-care, the soft life, and all that good stuff. We should definitely fix the things that we can and be committed to continuous growth and improvement. However, the simple truth is that we are all imperfect beings in one way or another. Chances are that nothing will ever totally be perfect in our lives. It may not be ideal, and going according to how you'd like.

What do we do then in response? Do we focus on what's imperfect and get stuck there? Or do we improve what we can, or even accept things as they are, and instead shift our focus to the more 'likeable' aspects? For example, in my case, I could choose to become fixated on what I see in my face and fingers that I don't like; become upset about it, and then fall into a downward spiral where I heap more negative self-thoughts and make myself feel even worse. Sounds fun, right? Or I could switch my attention to aspects such as my beautiful brown eyes and how much I love them (especially when I have makeup on).

Embrace your imperfections, know that they make you uniquely you. Be confident that you are enough, and while we may all need a bit of 'renovation' or maybe overdue for an 'upkeep maintenance', you are fine just the way you are! Self-love is of great importance, and the truth is, you owe it to yourself to love yourself just the way you are, imperfections and all!

It's OK to Retreat, Just DON'T Surrender!

There are numerous accounts in the Bible when Jesus took time away from the crowd so that He could PRAY. In Luk. 5:16, **Jesus WITHDREW himself to the wilderness to PRAY**. Certainly, most people have a daily prayer routine (or at least strive to). However, there are moments when the cares of life tend to become intensely overbearing, and praying seems to be just too hard to do. In these moments, we may become increasingly angered, frustrated, and even depressed. We may even become confused about what to do. What should my next move be? Where should I turn next? Some people may choose to confide in a friend (someone who often cannot even offer any real type of help) while others may engage in risky behaviours such as illicit sex, gambling, drug, and drinking addictions. Some people may even become ill due to stress and anxiety.

Looking to Jesus as an example may be beneficial if ever we feel like the walls of life are closing in on us. Take a moment to step back or even step away from any situation that seems to be weighing you down, RELAX - put some music on, light a candle, dance, play a game, go to the beach, take a walk, go to that secluded spot that makes your heart smile, AND PRAY! Doing this consistently can work wonders! As you quiet your mind, your fears begin to subside, anxiety levels lessen, and inner peace begins to flow. As you pray and meditate, burdens are rolled away, and we start to hear the voice of God as He instructs, gives directions, and opens doors on our behalf.

Praying is simply talking to God, just as we would with anyone else. We open up to Him, tell it all, and simply bear our souls in a space that is 100% safe. As you do this, you will literally feel the Peace of God start to flood you, and things that once bothered you dissipate like fog, and the bright and beautiful morning sun will begin to shine in.

Our RETREAT can be done right at home, in the office, before we head home, in the vehicle as we journey, or just about anywhere. From time to time, too, we may need to take a well-needed vacation or a getaway of some sort, TAKE A BREAK from the hustle and bustle of life, RETREAT- PRAY- MOVE AGAIN! Repeat when necessary! JUST DON'T SURRENDER!

Just Breathe – Everything Will Be FINE!

Have you ever been flustered? Maybe you have felt overwhelmed because of the insurmountable challenges that you are faced with. Perhaps you might have felt defeated because things aren't going the way that you want them to. You might have even cried yourself to sleep at night due to sadness and unmet needs. You long for a break. You wish for things to just be 'normal' even for a little while. But no, it's one issue after another; sometimes the problems even come in multiples. It's like you can't catch a break, and you feel weary and forlorn.

The good news is that you are not alone. God sees, and He knows, and even though you may sometimes feel that He has abandoned you - HE HAS NOT! There are numerous accounts in the bible where we see God showing up in some dire situations at the right time. Lazarus was in the tomb for four days (Joh 11); the woman with the issue of blood suffered for twelve long years (Luk 8:43-48); the widow of Nain was on the way to bury her only son (Luk. 7:11-17); Hannah was mocked by her antagonist (1 Sam. 1:6-2:1); the disciples thought that they would die in the tempestuous storm (Mrk 4:35-41); Elijah felt threatened by Jezebel, got depressed and ran into hiding (1 Kin. 19).

In each of these situations, the individuals must have experienced deep hopelessness; however, the outcomes of their stories stand as powerful testaments to the depth of our Heavenly Father's love and care for us because He brought victory to their lives. You and I are no different. God has not forgotten nor abandoned us. His word encourages us to **Take my yoke upon you…for my yoke is easy and my burden light** (Mat.11:29-30). Yokes and burdens are not things that we want attached to us, but we can be assured that yoking ourselves to the Great God, Creator of the universe, Lord of lords, The Great I Am, is very beneficial to us.

Trust and believe that He has all the fine details worked out. He is working behind the scenes for you. It may seem like all the odds are stacked against you, and you are about to go under, but just let go of the reins of your life and hand them over to the Lord, get out of the driver's seat, and let the Lord steer. Step back, submit everything to the master, and just BREATHE because everything will be fine. God's got you!

Look for the silver lining beyond the dark clouds.

Man that is born of a woman is of few days and full of trouble (Job 14:1). Based on this scripture, it is safe to conclude that for as long as we live, there will be some form of trouble in our lives. Being human and alive automatically qualifies us for trouble. Comforting, right? It's not a thought that we would like to bear at the forefront of our minds daily, but it is, in fact, a hard truth that we should be mindful of. So, since 'Man is full of trouble' (woman included), how do we navigate a life filled with trouble?

For starters, Psa. 46:1 boldly declares that **God is our refuge and strength, a very present help in trouble.** Therefore, while we might be full of trouble, we have help, and this is very reassuring! Trouble isn't permanent (2 Cor. 4:17, Psa. 30:5). Knowing this, then, we can take comfort knowing that whatever hardships and challenges we are faced with, they will come to an end. After every storm, there comes a calm. Some tough situations may seem as though they are only getting worse, but even the toughest of situations must yield at some point. The water receded steadily from the earth. At the end of the hundred and fifty days, the water had gone down (Gen 8:3). The earth had been flooded, and water was everywhere, BUT after 150 long days it began to recede and not just any old way! It began to recede STEADILY.

You may feel overwhelmed and outnumbered by the myriad of problems that bombard you; nonetheless, brighter days are ahead. Instead of dwelling on the problems and pressures of life, a shift in mindset and a posture of unshakeable faith in the abilities of God are needed. Especially in difficult times, we must change how we view problems and burdens. Remembering and declaring the word of God over every situation is optimal. There is a WORD for everything! Be it sickness, brokenness, disappointment, anxiety, stress - there is a scripture to apply and declare over it. Also, never forget that the prayer of a righteous person is powerful and effective (James 5:16). So, in the good and bad times, rejoice always, pray without ceasing, give thanks in all circumstances; for this is the will of God in Christ Jesus for you (1 Thes. 5:16-18).

Ask God to help you to see even the bad things through a positive lens while you bear Rom 8:28 in your heart - And we know that for those who love God all things work together for good, for those who are called according to his purpose. It's not just the good things that work together for good - it's all things, and this includes the bad things too. On days when you feel outnumbered by life's challenges, don't be afraid, for more are with you than those against you (Kin 6:16). Every dark cloud has a silver lining - even yours.

Time to Reflect

SECTION III: EMOTIONAL & MENTAL WELL-BEING

Thought Life • Emotional Regulation • Inner Battles • Mental Clarity • Peace

1. The Dangers of Overthinking

1. What situations cause me to overthink the most?
2. Are my thoughts based on truth, fear, or assumptions?
3. How can I redirect overthinking into prayer and intentional reflection?
4. What does it look like to trust God with what I can't control?

2. Dealing With Mental Overload

1. What responsibilities or expectations feel too heavy right now?
2. What can I release, delegate, or pause to protect my well-being?
3. Am I giving myself permission to rest?
4. What practices help my mind feel lighter?

3. Be Mindful of Your Reactions

1. What emotions influence my reactions the strongest?
2. Do I respond or react: what's the difference for me?

3. When do I feel most tested in my patience or self-control?

4. How can I create a pause between emotion and action?

4. Emotions Are Fickle — Beware!

1. Which emotions tend to lead me rather than follow God's truth?

2. How often do I make decisions based on temporary feelings?

3. What patterns do I notice in my emotional highs and lows?

4. How can I allow the Holy Spirit to regulate my emotions?

5. Embracing Our Imperfections

1.   Which imperfections do I criticize most within myself?

2.   How does God view these imperfections differently than I do?

3.   What would life feel like if I accepted myself fully?

4.   In what ways can I show myself more grace?

6. It's OK to Retreat, Just DON'T Surrender!

1.   What is draining me emotionally right now?

2.   Where do I need rest, not resignation?

3.   How can I practice stepping back without giving up?

4.   What does a healthy retreat look like for me?

7. Just Breathe — Everything Will Be FINE!

1.   What situations rob me of peace and calm?

2.   How does my body respond when I'm overwhelmed?

3.   What simple practices help me breathe and reset?

4.   How can I remind myself that "this too shall pass"?

8. Look for the Silver Lining Beyond the Dark Clouds

1. What challenges am I facing that may contain hidden blessings?
2. What positive shifts, lessons, or growth can I identify from past hardships?
3. How can gratitude shift my emotional atmosphere today?
4. What scripture anchors me when life feels heavy?

Section IV:

RISING IN STRENGTH & PURPOSE.

Confidence, Action, Boldness, Overcoming Obstacles, Spiritual Bravery.

"She is clothed with strength and dignity, and she laughs without fear of the future."

(Prov. 31:25)

There comes a moment when a woman realizes her strength, rises to her calling, and steps boldly into the life God designed for her.

This section challenges you to stretch, to grow, and to walk courageously in purpose.

These vials will remind you that strength is not loud or harsh but rather resilient, disciplined, and deeply rooted in faith.

You are called to rise, and this is the season to walk forward with confidence.

Winning Against All Odds

Everywhere we look, there seems to be an obstacle. These obstacles can be physical, emotional, financial, mental, cultural, among others. If we are not careful, we may become confounded by these obstacles and start to believe that we are not able to WIN. This is not so, though, even with the odds seemingly stacked against us, we can still WIN. **If God is for us, who can be against us?** (Rom. 8:31).

We meet a nameless woman in the Gospels (Matt. 9, Mrk. 5, Luk. 8). This woman is commonly referred to as 'The Woman with the issue of blood'. Her story is well known – she had a bleeding condition for twelve arduous years. She was broken physically, emotionally, financially, and – I believe – spiritually. She sought help, but everything seemed futile. I can imagine the toll that this condition took on her, especially living in that social context. Society expected her to be isolated due to her condition, but there was a WINNER deep within this woman that caused her to never lose hope.

This woman is symbolic of many women today who suffer from an infirmity that threatens to ruin their lives. However, just like The Woman with the issue of blood, we cannot allow the cares of life to overpower us because **"Greater is He that is in me, than he that is in the world"** (1 Joh. 4:4). She got word that Jesus was passing by, and she was confident that He was able to set her free. She did not allow the stigma of society, her brokenness, or her shame to deter her. She knew that all these odds were stacked against her. She also knew that she would literally have to push through the crowd to get to Jesus, and she was prepared to do just that because she knew that her healing was imminent.

What odds are you faced with today? They may seem like a mountain that you just cannot get past. Be reminded that if we have faith and not doubt, we can command mountains to move (Mrk 11:23). **Nothing is impossible with God** (Luk 1:37). The odds are real, but so is our God, and with Him on our side, we certainly can WIN against all odds – no matter what they are!

Let No Be Your Superpower

Are you afraid of telling people no? Especially when you are asked for something or for a favor. Do you feel 'some type of way' to tell people NO? And even if you do tell someone NO, do you then feel obligated to explain yourself? If you answered YES to at least some of those questions, then you are certainly not alone.

The truth is, we don't like to disappoint others (well, most people, I'd imagine). But what tends to happen is that sometimes when we fail to tell others NO, it is to our own detriment. The fact is that we sometimes do not think of the implications that our failure to say NO eventually has on us. Sometimes these implications are costly, whether financially, physically, spiritually, or otherwise. Failure to say no causes us to go above and beyond for others, and we may overexert our energy and overextend ourselves, and then leave ourselves in some amount of turmoil or predicament just because we did not carefully consider before offering up a delightful YES or a chirpy SURE! Many times, we recognize the danger and even become remorseful when it is much too late.

Now! Do not get me wrong. I am not at all suggesting that we be selfish and unhelpful just for the sake of it. Of course, we are to be our brother's keep! Certainly, we are to offer help and support to each other! What I am saying is, do not be too quick to agree to every request that comes your way. Take a moment and weigh the cost. Ask yourself questions such as: Do I have the time, resources, skills, and energy to comply with this request at this particular time? Do I even want to do this?

Nothing is wrong with saying NO. Saying NO does not make you a bad person. In fact, it is freeing, it is empowering, and it is necessary, and it is for us to be wise enough to decide when to utilize our superpower called NO.

NO Is An Answer

When we make a request of someone; the expectation is never to get the response 'NO'. The fact is, we have not been cultured to hear NO as the answer. However, NO is a very reasonable and sometimes necessary answer. Sometimes we need to hear NO, since it may be necessary to prevent us from accessing something that is not good for us. Human nature is to desire things that we perceive will make our lives better. Sometimes, though, our judgement might be clouded, and so we are unable to see the bigger picture.

Everyone is entitled to tell others NO, no matter who it is. Boundaries are important, and saying NO may be a way of protecting those boundaries. We want what we want, when we want, and how we want. However, when others are involved, what we want may not be in their best interest, and so, while it may be good for us, it may not be in their best interest, and so, their saying NO serves them best, and it is within their right to offer that response - whether we like it or not.

We may even take the same approach with God and pout at Him when He tells us NO. For instance, we may pray to God for specific things, and He, being All-Knowing, withholds what we have prayed for from us simply because it does not align with His perfect will for our lives, and so we may be left feeling as though 'God did not answer my prayer', when in fact He did. His answer was NO and NO, just like yes is a very valid response. We should graciously accept God's NO because if He tells us NO, it simply means that He has better in store for us.

Scriptures tell us that Eye has not seen, nor ear heard, neither have entered into the heart of man, the things which God hath prepared for them that love him (1 Cor. 2:9). We are also reminded that He is able to do exceedingly abundantly above all that we ask or think (Eph 3:20). Romans 8:28 also tells us that God works all things together for the good of those who love Him, who are called according to His purpose. Therefore, if God tells us NO, trust and believe that He has even better in store for you, and His no is not to punish you but to make room for an even greater blessing than your mind can fathom.

Surpass Challenges and Rise to the Occasion

Have you ever had something deep in your heart that you know expressly that it is the will of God for you to carry out? Even knowing this 'thing' is what God has mandated you to do, it still seems like an insurmountable task! You may start to wonder and ponder and make excuses. Laziness sets in, procrastination takes over! You may talk yourself out of it by finding all the excuses as to why this task, this dream, this calling is outside of your capacity to attain. The days, weeks, months, and even years roll by with you still feeling stuck! You might have even started, and things didn't go quite as planned. Perhaps you enthusiastically shared your dream with someone you love and trust, someone you were expecting to motivate you - to cheer you on. But that didn't happen! Instead, they fueled your doubt, convinced you even more that 'Yes, it really is a bad idea! You definitely can't do that!"

What if, however, you become resolute? You decide that, come what may, you are going to persevere! You do not have the money to finance this dream, you have no clue how you are going to accomplish such a great task, but you are determined that come-what-may, you are going to TRY! How about applying the wisdom that is found in Pro. 3:5 **"Trust in the LORD with all your heart and lean not on**

your own understanding" Let's go a little further and truly believe this verse from the Gospels **"With God nothing is impossible"** (Luk. 1:37, Luk. 18:27, Mar. 10:27, Matt. 19:26).

You see, we serve a God who really is **"above all things"** (Eph. 4:6, Heb. 1, Psa. 113:4-6) and He can do all things! Including supplying us with grace and favor to accomplish everything in our lives that is in accordance with His will. For starters, it requires faith! We must believe! But faith alone is by no means sufficient. As stated in Jas 2:26 "…**Faith without works is DEAD**". We have to put in the work! We have to stop feeding our minds with doubt! We have to push past laziness and quit delaying until circumstances become more favorable. Commit everything to prayer, dust off the dreams and visions that lie dormant in the corner. Time is crucial, and so we must maximize it.

By no means is this an encouragement to 'run ahead of God' nor to make reckless and foolish decisions that will cost us in the long run. It is about being sensitive to the Spirit of God and holding fast to the dreams and visions that he has embedded deep within you that run the risk of going unfulfilled! It is about having faith, not in our own abilities, but in the omnipotent power of our Everlasting King. It is knowing without a shadow of a doubt that indeed **"I can do all things through Christ who gives me strength"** (Phil. 4:13). This is what this is about!

Comfort Zone, The Enemy Of Growth

It might very well be human nature for us to feel comfortable and secure in a familiar environment. Being in a place that we are familiar with, be it physical or purely mental, can bring us comfort and even peace. We know just what to expect in that space - we feel in control, and who doesn't like this feeling? This often becomes our Comfort Zone - it's our domain, there, usually, there are no surprises since we know just what to expect. Usually, we know just what to expect there and that we can deal with. As for the uncertainty that lies beyond the walls of our comfort zone, we would rather not take the chance to explore.

The sad reality, though, is that while our Comfort Zone creates this habitat that acts as a safety net, it also erects walls that can be crippling. I remember this analogy of being a big fish in a small pond. In essence, that is what the comfort zones of many look like. Many would rather stay in the confines of the pond rather than risk the unknown of what lies in a lake or the wide ocean. Many have stopped dreaming because they have achieved 'much' and feel as though they have reached the limit on their potential. BUT, until we are dead, we still have more areas to grow in. In fact, many die with so much unreleased potential just because they have lingered in their comfort zones for far too long.

Comfort zones kill dreams; there, we talk ourselves out of further growth and advancements. We sit, and we ponder about everything that can, and probably will, go wrong. We convince ourselves that "I am ok - that is not for me, or I really don't need to do that." How about these ones: "I have nothing to prove", "I am not good enough", "I am going to fail", "I don't like change", "I am not a risk-taker". I could go on, but you get the gist.

Stepping out of the comfort zone takes courage, determination, and grit. By no means is it an easy feat to launch out into the unfamiliar. However, what lies on the other side of the walls of our comfort zones can be absolutely magical, life-changing, and just what our heart requires. Prayerfully, push yourself to get out of your comfort zone. Do not act blindly or impulsively but do move out of that comfort zone because you were built for more.

The Road of Success is Lined With Gold

Success is one of those things that many people aspire towards. However, what is success? Success may look like different things for different individuals. For some, success may be landing their dream job, getting married, migrating to a first-world country, or any of the myriad of other achievements that society has prescribed for success. For me, however, success is more of a process than it is an end product or achievement. Put it this way, I much prefer the concept of a "Successful Life".

Imagine a road from your birth to death. Now think of this road from one end to the other as SUCCESS. Along this road, you may encounter exhilarating moments that bring you joy and much happiness. On the flip side, you may encounter pain and anguish that cause you to cry and be in despair. However, still see this journey as one worthy of being called SUCCESSFUL, because you see – Life is not all about the 'peaches and cream' that novels and movies teach us. Life includes some tough moments, some unpleasant times; things that are meant to squish us. Even these moments are purposeful, though. They holistically work together to build character and grit as well as to teach us valuable lessons (if we are indeed desirous of learning).

Now imagine this road of SUCCESS being lined with **G.O.L.D**: -

Gratitude – Always be grateful along each step of the way

Be **O**riginal – Be your authentic self. Remember, God made you special!

Love, Laugh, Live, be **Loyal** – Have a positive attitude no matter what!

Be **D**etermined – Never give up! Keep pushing! Trod on!

As you pursue this SUCCESSFUL LIFE, here are some tips that you may find useful:

1. Find out what drives you. Ask yourself: What is my passion, and how can I ignite it?

2. Make a plan and stick to it!

3. Assess your progress regularly

4. Re-plan if necessary

5. Be prepared for struggles. Remember, nothing comes easily

6. Believe in yourself. Be determined. If you can dream it, you can achieve it

7. Use stumbling blocks as stepping stones

8. Be purposeful. Seek out resources and new opportunities

9. Be inspired by great individuals. Model mountain climbers – they require tenacity and resilience.

10. Remember – no matter who you are, where you are from, what your past or current circumstances are – WITH GOD YOU CAN MAKE IT!

11. Always be reflective. Thank those who helped along your journey.

12. Be deliberate about inspiring others. Help others as much as you possibly can

Remember! Continuously and consistently consult God, ask Him if it is His will for your life. Ask Him to open the eyes of your understanding that you may be able to fully follow His lead as he directs your path. Meditate on Pro. 3: 5-6 **Trust in the Lord with ALL of thine heart and lean not to thine own understanding but in all thy ways acknowledge Him and He shall direct thy path.**

Also, bear in mind that even though you may have what you believe is the perfect plan, God is sovereign and His plans for your life far supersede any plan that you may conjure up.

As you pursue your SUCCESSFUL LIFE, bear the following scriptures in mind:

Psa. 37:23 - **The steps of a good man are ordered by the Lord: and he delighteth in his way**

Pro. 19:21 - **Many are the plans in a person's heart, but it is the LORD's purpose that prevails.** (NIV)

Matt. 6:10 **Thy kingdom come. Thy will be done on earth, as it is in heaven.**

HAVE A SUCCESSFUL LIFE, FRIENDS!

Reach for the strength of the Proverbs 31 woman within you

A fundamental truth that I have come to realize in recent years is this: 'Being a woman is by no means an easy feat'. In general, women face many challenges, obstacles, trials, and situations. There are both physical and emotional hardships that women face that cause even further distress. Then, there are the personal, professional, and social expectations that women must meet. Like I already pointed out, being a woman is difficult! This is not by any means an attempt to discredit the challenges that men face. The focus here is on the female experience.

Despite the challenges, though, there is still a champion inside; a warrior; a winner, and she can come forth. It can be daunting sometimes to dig deep within to muster up the strength to 'show up', to thrive, and to excel in life. However, Rom. 8:37 reminds us that "**in all these things we are more than conquerors through him who loved us**". The reality is that life presents insurmountable challenges, but the truth is that amidst our life's challenges, "**God is our refuge and strength**" (Psa. 46:1). With courage and determination, we can overcome obstacles.

If we direct our attention to the events that are happening around us in the world, we will undoubtedly encounter a wide range of opinions, programs, and formulas for success. Nonetheless, scriptures provide us with an excellent example of a woman whom we can all emulate if we want to be successful according to God's ordinances for our lives. This example is found in Prov. 31. This chapter is commonly known; however, it's worth being examined closely and diligently. This virtuous woman has so many qualities that we cannot just admire but also replicate in our own lives.

She is smart, thoughtful, wise, strong, industrious, and resourceful, among so many other things. She prioritizes the needs of her household and puts measures in place to ensure that they are well taken care of. Even though she is married, evidence from the scripture proves that she does not solely depend on her husband. In fact, she comes alongside him and offers support. She understands God's initial design of a woman to be a helpmate (Gen. 2:18). Certainly, her role as a wife, mother, entrepreneur, and leader, among other things, must have been difficult at times. Even though the scriptures make no mention of this concerning the woman described in Proverbs 31, I am sure there must have been days when, like you and I, she felt tired and possibly overwhelmed. She was no superwoman, and neither are you, but she carried supernatural grace, and so do you. The key is to tap into this grace that is well up on the inside of each of us. So, my friend, my sister, I implore you to reach for the strength of the Proverbs 31 woman that is within you.

Maximizing on the Time NOW

We all have big dreams and visions that we wish to accomplish. We have been carrying some of them from as far back as our childhood days. Life doesn't pause; it's a constant GO. The older we become, the more responsibilities we have, and it seems like there is less time to work on bringing our dreams to reality. Sometimes we even make the mistake of thinking that now is not the right time, or we await an ideal time when our circumstances are more conducive. I absolutely understand that some things happen within the 'perfect time'. However, there is also great value in maximizing the time that we have now.

We can sometimes feel as though there is not enough time to work on that goal that we carry. However, quite often, so much time is lost waiting for the 'right time' to come around. Instead, doing small deliberate actions in increments can make a huge advance for us a far way instead of waiting around for the ideal time to accomplish a huge chunk in one go.

There is an adage that says, "Do not put off for tomorrow what you can do today." This saying carries immense wisdom. Sometimes the problem isn't that there isn't enough time, but more so that we lack discipline, commitment, and consistency in doing what is required to get us where we desire to go. Normally, especially at the beginning of the year, we outline numerous plans that we wish to achieve.

However, unless these plans are backed by DOING, then they're all futile. If we are not intentional and put in the necessary work, then months and even years will pass by whilst we remain stagnant and fixed on awaiting our circumstances to align perfectly. The truth is, though, that may never happen.

It is therefore very prudent to utilize our time wisely, because it is very true that time wasted can never be regained. Think about it, we can no longer access yesterday, last week, or last year. Those times are forever gone like the water that flows along a rushing stream. There is a lot of value in NOW, so use it to your advantage. You definitely won't regret it and will for sure thank yourself someday in the future.

Maintain Your Focus - Don't Mind The Distractors

There are distractions all around us. Our phones are constantly going off with notifications from the numerous apps that are loaded on them. It seems as though there is always some news trending on social media that we believe we definitely have to see. Then, there are the friends and family members whom we don't see as often as we would like and want to catch up with. Obligations at work, home, church, in the community - I could go on.

There are so many things competing for our attention, yet there are some essential things that the Lord requires of us that, if we are not very careful, might get left undone by the wayside. You see, time is a very precious commodity that, once wasted, is unrecoverable. While we can work harder to 'make up time,' it is best to be mindful of how we spend our time to begin with. To avoid this, we must be purposeful and intentional with our time.

Distractions can be a master stealer of our time. They are subtle and cunning, yet they cause us to lose so much time without us even recognizing it. A major type of distraction to pay attention to is the people who come to remove our focus from our important tasks. They appear in the form of a friendly conversation, a plea for help with their own tasks, an innocent invite to join them at an event - one you had no plans to attend. Without even noticing, we get absorbed into whatever it is that they have diverted our attention to, and time quickly rolls by.

When Nehemiah undertook the project to rebuild Jerusalem's walls, his opponents tried to distract him. In fact, they made deliberate attempts to get Nehemiah's attention away from this project (Neh. 6). Nehemiah responded with wisdom and did not fall for their bait, and remained steadfast in what he was doing. The result was that the arduous task of rebuilding the walls was completed in record time, in just 52 days. Imagine if Nehemiah had fallen for the trick of his adversaries!

Like Nehemiah, we too have to be aware of the numerous distractions and distractors around us. No, it does not mean that we are going to shun people altogether. It simply means that we are to maintain our focus in moments when it matters most so that we can get important tasks done. That may mean shutting off our televisions, not answering a phone call, not accepting an invitation; discerning what the distractions are, and avoiding them.

Time to Reflect

SECTION IV: RISING IN STRENGTH & PURPOSE

Confidence • Action • Boldness • Overcoming Obstacles •

Spiritual Bravery

Winning Against All Odds

1. What odds am I facing right now that make my journey feel difficult?

2. How has God empowered me to overcome challenges in the past?

3. What would "victory" look like in this situation?

4. What mindset shift do I need to win with grace and faith?

---

2. Let NO Be Your Superpower

1. What have I been saying "yes" to that drains my strength or purpose?

2. In what ways am I afraid to say "no?"

3. How can saying "no" become an act of self-respect and obedience to God?

4. What boundaries do I need to strengthen right now?

3. NO Is an Answer

1. Why do I feel obligated to explain or justify my boundaries?

2. How does God model healthy boundaries in Scripture?

3. Where do I need to stand firm without guilt?

4. What freedom comes from embracing simplicity in my decisions?

4. Surpass Challenges and Rise to the Occasion

1. What current challenge is actually an invitation from God to rise higher?

2. What strengths have I developed through adversity?

3. How can I prepare myself mentally and spiritually to rise when called?

4. Who benefits when I choose to rise to the occasion instead of shrinking back?

5. The Road of Success Is Lined With GOLD

1. What "GOLD" (Gratitude, Originality, Love, Determination) do I need to cultivate more?

2. How do I define success from a spiritual perspective?

3. What beliefs or behaviors keep me from progressing on my God-ordained path?

4. What would make my journey toward success more joyful and intentional?

---

6. Reach for the Strength of the Proverbs 31 Woman Within You

1. What qualities of the Proverbs 31 woman do I see in myself already?

2. What characteristics do I desire to grow in?

3. How can I become more intentional about living with dignity, competence, and purpose?

4. What does "strength and honor" look like in my everyday life?

7. Maximizing On The Time NOW

1. How much of my current time aligns with my true priorities and God-given assignments?

2. Where am I procrastinating, and why?

3. What opportunities is God calling me to maximize instead of delay?

4. What habits can help me be more intentional and productive?

8. Maintain Your Focus – Don't Mind the Distractors

1. What are the biggest distractions in my life right now?

2. How can I ground myself in God's Word to stay focused?

3. What does "laser-like focus" look like for my purpose?

4. How can I respond to distractions with grace and maturity?

Section V:

TRUST, DISCIPLINE & DIVINE ALIGNMENT.

Faith, Waiting, Obedience, Surrender, Discernment.

"Trust in the Lord with all your heart and lean not on your own understanding."

(Prov. 3:5)

Walking with God requires trust: trust in His timing, His silence, His guidance, and His ways.

This section invites you to cultivate spiritual discipline and align your steps with His direction.

Even when the path seems uncertain, know that God is leading, shaping, and preparing you.

These vials will strengthen your faith and encourage you to surrender fully to His perfect plan.

God's Blueprint For YOU

Most people are very familiar with Je. 1:5 where God declares to Jeremiah that **"Before I formed thee in the belly I knew thee; and before thou camest forth out of the womb I sanctified thee, and I ordained thee a prophet unto the nations."** For sure, God knew the plan that He had for Jeremiah long before he was even conceived! Just like Jeremiah, our destinies have been carefully crafted out by the Creator - every intricate detail has been worked out long before we came into existence. Do not let the enemy deceive you into harboring thoughts such as "Yes, my destiny of doom has already been signed off on, so why bother?" Let's go back to Jeremiah for a moment; his immediate response to God was, "I do not know how to speak; I am too young." Straight away, he started to give excuses as to why he would not be able to fulfil his God given assignment. To that, God simply reassured him by saying, "Do not be afraid of them, for I am with you and will rescue you". Let's imagine for a moment that Jeremiah had continued with his excuses and just simply refused to go "to nations and kingdoms to uproot and tear down, to destroy and overthrow, to build and to plant". My thinking is that God would have eventually left him alone, and for sure, Jeremiah's destiny would have been different.

Like Jeremiah, we were all created for a purpose that preexisted us. Yes! Our purpose was crafted long before we even came into existence. Think of your dream house. You know all the fine details that you want in it, right? From how many rooms to the type of lighting fixtures to the type of countertops. EVERY DETAIL. Before the house is even constructed, there has to be a Blueprint with all the details clearly outlined. If followed with precision, then the expectation is that the house will turn out just the way it was intended. There are, however, times when mistakes are made during construction, the budget may run out, or there may be some other unforeseen circumstance that can affect the finished product. So is it with our lives. But should we just give up on our house? I say NO! Take a break, perhaps, and Seek out other options. Try to figure out something else. JUST DON'T GIVE UP!

We, like houses, all have a blueprint that was crafted by God, the Master Builder. If followed with precision, then there is no doubt that our lives will be purposeful and fulfilling. Undoubtedly, there will be challenges along the way. It will not always be smooth sailing. Circumstances will not always be ideal. Maybe things get stalled in your life for a while. However, keep pushing knowing that you were created with a purpose and that once your life is fully surrendered to Christ, then there is nothing (or no one) that can effectively stop you from living a successful life.

God has a blueprint for you. I go back to the analogy of building a house. Perhaps you are at the stage where your foundation is being dug out or erected. Maybe blocks are being laid gently, one on top of the other. Perhaps your roofing is being installed, or you are at the stage where decorative finishes are being put in. You may even feel like you are an old house that has been left uncared for and in desperate need of refurbishment. Wherever you are in your process, never lose sight of the fact that every intricate detail of your life matters to God. After all, **"the very hairs of your head are all numbered"** so **"Don't be afraid; you are worth more than many sparrows."** (Luk. 12:17). Again, WHAT A BLESSED ASSURANCE!

Be gentle to yourself; remember that every great edifice takes time to become a great masterpiece. So, while you are being built, know that you still have a purpose in every phase and stage of your life. There are also different architectural styles; therefore, do not compare yourself to the 'building' next to you. Truth is, there will always be a more elaborate 'building' than yours, but that does not diminish the value and purpose that you hold. Your walls may be due for a fresh coat of paint, and some maintenance work is needed in your roof, but still, you serve a purpose and can be repaired and restored - for His glory.

Stay prayed up as you pursue your God-given assignment on this earth. And if you are yet to discover it, with sincere prayer, I know for sure that you will come face to face with your purpose/destiny. Remember, you are not a mistake. God is definitely too perfect to make mistakes. He created you with great plans in mind and is watching over you to ensure that they come to pass.

There is Purpose in Your WAITING

Have you ever been desperately waiting for something? Something that you so badly want, but it all seems elusive. You so badly want this thing that it occupies your every waking thought. You perhaps even dream about it at night. In short, you want this thing so badly that it is truly consuming you! You might have done all that you know how to, and you have done it well. You have prayed and fasted. You have fasted and prayed again, but still nothing! To top it all off, God might have even spoken and confirmed to you that this is something that is in His divine will for you. But why isn't it happening? Why can't I obtain it?

Certainly, this is a difficult place to be. For many, it's a place of distress and despondency; a place of hopelessness and despair. It's in these moments, however, that we must dig deeper and truly pursue God even more. This may not be what you wish to hear (well-read), but there is purpose in your waiting. It's during these times that God truly builds our character, resilience, and understanding while He increases our depth in Him. It's a time for growth and expansion spiritually. Imagine the flip side of not having to wait - where everything that you desire is granted instantaneously. Sounds like a spoiled child, right? No lessons learned, a sense of entitlement, just smooth sailing through life.

Don't be mistaken, some things will come quickly - in accordance with how God allows them to manifest. BUT there will definitely be those times when He causes us to WAIT so that He can be glorified - Remember Lazarus, his friend? So, during the wait, how about we change our posture? How about we look beyond what we are so eagerly awaiting and seek to understand the valuable lesson God is teaching us during this season? Several scriptures speak expressly about God's expectation of us while we wait on Him.

But they that wait upon the Lord shall renew their strength; they shall mount up with wings as eagles; they shall run and not be weary; and they shall walk, and not faint. Isa. 40:31

Be anxious for nothing, but in everything by prayer and supplication, with thanksgiving, let your requests be made known to God; 7 and the peace of God, which surpasses all understanding, will guard your hearts and minds through Christ Jesus (Phil. 4:6-7).

Wait on the Lord be of good courage, and he shall strengthen thine heart: wait, I say, on the Lord (Psa. 27:14).

I could quote more scriptures, but I believe you get the point. So, I encourage you to take courage; allow God to work in your life as you wait. Seek to find His will and try to learn that which He wishes to teach you while you wait. For here's the truth, that which we so desperately await will not come a minute sooner than God will allow it to. So, we might as well find joy and purpose in our season of waiting. Isa. 60:22 (b) sums it all up **"I am God. At the right time I'll make it happen"**.

Learn From the Journey: The Outcome Has Already Been Established

J er. 29:11 reads **"For I know the plans I have for you,"** declares the Lord, "plans to prosper you and not to harm you, plans to give you hope and a future. Wow! What an assurance! It almost sounds like we could take that to the bank! We have a heavenly Father who cares deeply for us, and He has only the best in store for us.

The problem though, is that He will at times give us directives and place things within our hearts that may seem very far-fetched. It is human nature for us to want details. We like knowing just how things will play out. That's not how it is with God, though. Think back to when He called Abraham, for example (Gen. 12). He simply told Abraham to leave His homeland, but He did not give him much more information. He did, however, make him some promises of what He would do for him, but He did not tell him the HOW.

This is a powerful example to everyone to simply be obedient to the voice of God and to move at His command, knowing that the end has already been established and it is GOOD! God already has it all figured out. He has worked out all the small details. The process that it takes to get there may be difficult; it might be riddled with numerous obstacles. We may feel as though we just do not have the wherewithal to make it, but the Lord will give us the strength to go on, and He will provide guidance along the way. Also, He will supply all the resources that we are in need of. After all, He owns the cattle on a thousand hills (Psa. 10:50).

We sometimes get very caught up with just getting to the end and overlook the process. There are a lot of lessons to learn while on the journey to the outcome. Character is developed, valuable lessons are learned, wisdom is imparted, knowledge increases, perspectives are broadened, and understanding expands as we undertake life's journeys. Know that there is value in the process that we all can benefit from; it refines us. The end is only the product, so do not wait until you get there to glean all the benefits. Prayerfully ask the Lord to reveal to you the hidden gems that He has along the way for you so that you can receive the blessings from them instead of waiting to get to the end - wherever that is.

You Are NOT Alone!

It's amazing how small isolated instances can all add together and be a grand blessing to the soul and spirit. After speaking to my husband late last night, my two-year-old phone died. Despite all my efforts to restart it, the phone would not budge! I thought, "Oh well, that's the end of the phone!" I kept on trying all morning, but all my efforts were still futile! I was therefore forced to use my house phone to make a call. Beside the telephone was a little devotional book called *The NLT BIBLE Promise Book.* I randomly turned a few pages until my eyes caught a scripture under the subtopic TEMPTATION.

1 Cor. 10:13 (NLT) **The temptations in your life are no different from what others experience. And God is faithful. He will not allow the temptation to be more than you can stand. When you are tempted, he will show you a way out so that you can endure.**

The KJV translation of this scripture reads **There hath no temptation taken you but such as is common to man: but God is faithful, who will not suffer you to be tempted above that ye are able; but will with the temptation also make a way to escape, that ye may be able to bear it.**

What is the connection with the phone? So, as I continued trying to turn the phone on, it dawned on me to try and Google the problem (I truly believe that this thought was inspired by the Holy Spirit). For a split second, I thought, "Naa, there is no way that I could Google a solution for this issue. The phone is dead!" Anyway, I felt compelled to proceed. After all, I could only gain. There was nothing to lose! And VOILA, in the very first search result, I found a solution, and my phone that was DEAD came back on within a minute or so!

It turns out that I was not the only one who had experienced that particular problem with the type of phone that I had. So, while I was thinking that my phone was dead because it is old, that was not so! On top of that, others have experienced the same issue, and MY PROBLEM WAS NOT UNIQUE.

So it is in life, sometimes we may encounter a problem, a conflict, a temptation, or carry a burden that we think we are the only one who is having such an experience. As a result, we may become disheartened and begin to reason within ourselves that certainly this will never go away because I AM THE ONLY ONE WITH THE ISSUE. Not so! According to God's word, everything we face, there are others who have faced this issue, are facing it, or will face it, and GOD HAS A SOLUTION!

It can be such a relief when we find out that "Oh, I am not the only one who has ever…." Instantly, we feel better knowing that we are not alone. The truth is, we were never alone. God is always with us. He has pledged **never to leave us nor to forsake us!** (Heb. 13:5). So, while you face your situation, remember:

1. Your issue is not unique to you! So don't beat yourself up and become hopeless!

2. God is faithful! He always was, always is, and always will be faithful! It's who He is! It's a part of His character!

3. God will not allow whatever you are facing to get the better of you!

4. There is a way of escape! There is hope! Just trust Him

5. While you go through whatever you do, He will give you the strength to bear it!

Remember, **His grace is sufficient!** (2 Cor. 12:9)

6. There is a solution for all you face! Wait patiently and prayerfully

Trusting Totally in God

Trust God' is a term that is used quite a lot, and if you ask me, it is used very loosely. So much so that it has become somewhat of a cliché. However, what does trusting God entail? What does it truly look like? Believe me, it is more than paying 'lip service'. Trusting God requires FAITH! That is the unshakeable confidence that God not only CAN, but that He WILL! It's believing with all certainty that, despite what our circumstances presently look like, God will show up on the scene, and He will work things out in our favor.

Actually, trusting God is far easier said than done. To fully trust God demands that we overcome the mental battle that rages in our minds. Crossing over the battle line from doubt to trust can be an arduous task. We must stop focusing on our problems and convincing ourselves just how dreadful and complicated they are, and instead turn our focus squarely towards our All-Powerful God. It requires a deep understanding and acknowledgment of who God is and His sovereign capabilities - there is nothing outside of His scope. He can do ALL things, and that includes - for you too! Trusting God totally is to believe this with all your heart (Prov. 3:5). Trusting God calls for an awareness that we can never truly figure out what God is up to concerning us, while at the same time resting in the assurance that His plans and intentions towards us are GOOD! (Jer. 29:11), and in His perfect timing, He will cause them to manifest and cause everything to come into alignment (Isa. 60:22).

Trusting God completely requires that we sometimes let go of everything that we hold dear and once considered to be true. It's knowing that our reality isn't finality. Even when the evidence that is presented to us tells us that "it is what it is", it's knowing that our God is more than capable of changing these circumstances instantaneously. (Matt. 8:23-27). On the other hand, Heb. 11:1 tells us that **even when there is no evidence of what we so desire, it is there!** That's faith and trusting in God. Therefore, even when we cannot figure out what God is doing, when we cannot understand His methods, we should still TRUST HIM!

For sure, we can depend on God. This dependency brings sweet peace and relief to our souls. Be resolute and unwavering when trusting God, having complete confidence in Him. Remember that trust and doubt cannot coexist. There is no such thing as trusting God 99%! Trust tainted with even a tinge of doubt is unbelief. So, do yourself a favor and TRUST totally in God.

When God Goes Silent

as God ever gone silent on you? You are praying, fasting, seeking, and NOTHING! NADA! ZIT! ZERO! You don't feel His presence; it's like He is far away from you. It's even worse if you are facing an adverse situation and need Him right now, but you seemingly just cannot perceive Him. You may even begin to question how connected you are spiritually. Why aren't you just not hearing from Him, especially now in a crucial moment? Whilst going through his afflictions, Job lamented, **On the left hand, where he doth work, but I cannot behold him: he hideth himself on the right hand, that I cannot see him'** (Job 23:9). At the lowest point in his life, Job expressed his frustration that God seemingly had gone silent on him. We might have a similar experience like Job - at a low point, seeking God and not being able to 'hear' from Him.

Since we are human and our scope of understanding is limited, it is not surprising that we may interpret God's silence even as a sign of Him abandoning us. However, we should be mindful that God's ways are higher than our ways and His thoughts higher than our thoughts (Isa. 55:8-9). We must understand, too, that God is sovereign, and He is not subjected to our every beck and call. He is all-knowing and knows the end from the beginning. His scope far outweighs ours, and His wisdom is beyond anything we could ever attain.

Knowing the nature of God, though, will serve as a major source of confidence for us during times when we cannot perceive Him - in moments when He is silent. Us not being able to 'hear from God' or to sense His presence does not in any way change who God is and what He is capable of accomplishing in our lives, and we should never forget this. His word affirms that He will never leave you nor forsake you (Duet. 31:8; Heb. 13:5). Just know that the Good Lord never sleeps nor slumbers (Psa. 121:4) nor does he take vacations. Psalm 34:15 tells us that the eyes of the LORD are on the righteous, and his ears are attentive to their cry.

Even though God may be silent, remember that He is right there with you, and when it suits him, He will speak life into your situation. An important point to note is that God being silent does not give us the right to be silent. No matter what, we should never cease to communicate with our Lord and Savior. Be confident that as long as we are speaking to Him, He will speak back to us.

So, God Has Granted Your Request, Now What?

You have fasted, you have prayed, you have cried, you prayed some more, and fasted for even longer. You wholeheartedly believe Matt. 7:7 that says Ask, and it shall be given you; seek, and ye shall find; knock, and it shall be opened unto you. You have diligently prayed, trusted, and believed, and finally - you have seen results - your prayers have been answered. Now what?

Has the fervency died, or is the zest still there? Is what you prayed for all that you anticipated? How do you treat the precious answer to your prayer - whatever it is? It is a blessing to be living in our answered prayer. It is a joy to see the manifestation of our prayers right before our eyes. A word of caution, though - When we begin to live in our answered prayers, we should not take for granted what we now have, nor lose the fervency with which we prayed to have what we now have or be where we now are. In fact. In fact, we must never allow ourselves to forget when we diligently interceded, begged God, cried out to Him for Him to grant us the desires of our hearts. Unfortunately, people sometimes end up treating our blessings with scant regard simply because they have forgotten that they came through prayer.

Here's a revelation to ponder on - What we have received through prayer requires prayer to maintain it, it needs prayer to keep it, and protect it. So, if you have prayed for and received - a spouse, a child, a house, a job, a (fill-in-the-blank)- it is going to take prayer to keep it. It requires consistent prayer to cover all that God has blessed us with. Like Luk. 18:1 reminds us - men ought always to pray, and not to faint". So, even when our prayers have been answered, we still have to pray without ceasing (1 Thes. 5:17). Our answered prayers need nurturing in the form of continued prayers that can unlock even greater blessings and breakthroughs. Therefore, when your prayers have been answered, it's not time to stop praying, but instead, it is time to PRAY. Pray on my friends.

Also, do not forget to praise and thank God for answering your prayers with the same fervor and urgency with which you prayed. Do not let the prayer request lists be lengthier than our praise reports and thanksgiving. If we are not careful, we may overlook God's goodness towards us and not return thanks unto Him when He has shown up miraculously in our situations. Remember the lepers who Jesus healed - of the ten, only one returned to praise Him for healing him, while the other nine continued on their merry way (Luke 17:11-19). Do not take anything that God does for you for granted - big or small (especially the small). Be deliberate about thanking and praising God while continuing in prayer once your prayers have been answered.

Time to Reflect

SECTION V: TRUST, DISCIPLINE & DIVINE ALIGNMENT
Faith • Surrender • Waiting • Obedience • Guidance •

God's Timing

1. There Is Purpose in Your WAITING

1. What am I waiting on God for right now?

2. How does my attitude during the waiting season reflect my faith?

3. What might God be developing in me through this period of delay?

4. How can I grow in patience and trust?

2. You Are NOT Alone!

1. When have I felt abandoned or forgotten—and what truth reassures me I am not alone?

2. How has God shown His presence in subtle or unexpected ways?

3. Who has God placed in my life as support during hard seasons?

4. How can I stay connected to God even when I feel isolated?

---

3. Trusting Totally in God

1. What fears make it difficult for me to trust God completely?

2. Where am I still trying to control outcomes instead of surrendering them?

3. What truth about God's character do I need to cling to right now?

4. How can I remind myself daily that God is trustworthy?

---

4. When God Goes Silent

1. When have I experienced a "silent season" with God?

2. What emotions surface when I feel like God is quiet?

3. What can silence teach me about patience, faith, and spiritual maturity?

4. How can I continue to pursue God even when I don't feel Him?

5. So, God Has Granted Your Request — Now What?

1. What blessing has God recently given that I need to steward well?

2. Am I honoring God with what He entrusted to me?

3. How do I ensure gratitude and obedience follow God's answered prayers?

4. What next step is God prompting me to take now that the door has opened?

Section VI:

LIVING WITH WISDOM
&
GRACE

STEWARDSHIP, GENEROSITY, SPIRITUAL MATURITY, PRACTICAL CHRISTIAN LIVING.

"Wisdom is the principal thing; therefore get wisdom."

(Prov. 4:7)

A winning woman does more than survive; she thrives by applying wisdom, carrying herself with grace, and making choices guided by the Holy Spirit.

In this section, you will learn practical and spiritual principles that shape a balanced, fulfilling, and purposeful life.

As you journey through these vials, may you grow in discernment, stewardship, generosity, and grace: tools that are essential for victorious and intentional living.

What Kind Of Steward Are You?

God expects us to treat with care and love everything that He has entrusted to us. We may take for granted the blessings that the Lord has bestowed upon us and even treat the things we have and the people in our lives with scant regard. Let's honestly reflect on the things and people in our lives. How are we treating them? Is God smiling when He looks down and sees how we treat our family members, friends, and possessions, or is He frowning? Are we utilizing the gifts, talents, and resources that he has bestowed upon us for His glory, or are we selfishly hoarding them only for personal gratification and self-glory? Are we selfish with our knowledge and wisdom, or do we joyfully share them with those around us?

All that God has entrusted to us -great and small- He expects us to be good stewards over them. The parable of the Ten Talents (Matt. 25: 14-30; Luk. 19: 11-17) is often used whenever the topic of stewardship is spoken about. This parable adequately teaches how to steward what God has given to us, not to merely tuck it away but to utilize it in a way that blesses others. This parable isn't just about being able to make wise financial investments that will multiply. It can be applied to just about every facet of our lives. Contemplate on this verse - As every man hath received the gift, even so minister the same one to another, as good stewards of the manifold grace of God.

(1 Pet. 4:10). It is clear - our gift/talent/blessing isn't merely for ourselves. It is to bless others.

For instance, you are blessed with the 'talent/gift' of encouraging others. Being a good steward of that gift may involve using it to bless others and even inspire people so much that they, too, become encouragers. Everything that God gives to us is intentional, and he requires us to take the absolute best care of it. Also, how we care for what we have determines whether or not the Lord will reward us with more 'talents'. Take a survey, how are your talents? Have you truly been a good steward? Can God reward you with more? Or will He reprove you and call you "Thou wicked and slothful servant"? (Matt. 25:26). The choice is yours!

Biblical Financial Principles You Can Trust

It is often said that 'money makes the world go round'. Financial burden can be such a stressor for many. From what we see around us, it seems that there is never enough money. The rich, no matter how much money they have, want more. Not to mention the poor and less fortunate. The bible makes note in Eccl. 10:19 that "money answers all things". All the necessities that we need in life require some amount of money, and the more comfortable and luxurious we desire our lives to be, the more money we will need. For many, a question at the forefront of their minds is "Can I truly live a financially stable life?" and if so, HOW? While I may not have the formula for how to be financially stable, there are biblical principles that, if adhered to diligently, can combat poverty and lack in our lives and cause a complete turnaround in our financial situation.

First is the principle of tithing. Essentially, this is giving back 10% of what we have earned. Some may say, "But I cannot even survive with 100% of what I currently earn," and to that I would say that is the reason to give to God your 10% so that he can, in turn, multiply your 90%. If we carefully examine Mal. 3:10-11, there is so much that we could glean from it. Let's take a look.

10. Bring ye all the tithes into the storehouse, that there may be meat in mine house, and prove me now herewith, saith the Lord of hosts, if I will not open you the windows of heaven, and pour you out a blessing, that there shall not be room enough to receive it.

11. And I will rebuke the devourer for your sakes, and he shall not destroy the fruits of your ground; neither shall your vine cast her fruit before the time in the field, saith the Lord of hosts.

I do hope that scripture made you excited! I encourage you to zoom in and carefully meditate on, especially the underlined promises that God makes. Remember, He's not a man who should lie.

Next, we have the principle of giving. In Acts 20:35, the Apostle Paul reminds us that 'It is more blessed to give than to receive.' I am sure that I am not the only one who likes to receive things. Let's be honest now! However, it is a scriptural principle that there are more benefits to be derived from giving than from receiving. You may argue, 'How can I give when what I have is not enough to supply my needs?' And to this I say, examine the Widow of Zarephath in 1 Kin. 17, who was facing harsh poverty but still made the sacrifice to use her last possession to bake Elijah a cake. The result - a miracle, she had enough to sustain herself and her sons. You don't need to have in abundance to give. Give, even if all you have is the widow's mite (Luk. 21:1-4).

The final principle I wish to point out is that of investing wisely and stewarding our possessions well. Let's look at the parable of the ten talents where different servants were given different amounts of money to steward until their master returned (Matt. 25:14-30). The outcome is that all but 1 servant had returns on the money when the master returned. They made wise financial decisions that caused the money to increase. The one servant who simply returned what he was given was chastised for not being a good steward. A great takeaway from this parable is that we should strive to make wise financial decisions that will bring an increase to our finances instead of causing them to diminish. Seek God to show ways to be a good steward over what he has entrusted us with, our money included. The truth is, many people have enough money but make the dire mistake of not stewarding it well. So, let's do some self-check. How much do you save from your earnings? Have I made WISE investments, or did I act on a whim? What God inspired ideas can help me generate and keep more money? Am I spending on necessities, or do I squander carelessly?

One last caution: be mindful that we have an adversary who wants to keep us bound. So, he will come and whisper lies about why we should not tithe, give, or be good stewards. Please, dispel the voice of the enemy because he means us no good and wants to keep us forever locked in a cycle of lack. Instead, choose to listen to the voice of God and abide by His principles, and watch yourself break free financially.

Find Joy in Giving

There can be many demands for our financial resources that can make things challenging for us. The bills are constant, emergencies pop up, and home and car repairs seem to be ever-present. At the same time, we may look around us and see various needs that require financial help. Some may either turn a blind eye to these situations or immediately begin to feel bad because they are unable to help. How can we possibly help when we are barely getting by? A biblical principle, despite our circumstances, is that you must **support the weak** (Acts 20:35). This same verse goes on to point out that it is more blessed to give than to receive (Acts 20:35).

Who doesn't like to receive things, though? For sure, I like to be on the receiving end. While we like to receive things, it is a blessing when we give. Think about it, which would you rather, to feel happy or to know that you are blessed for doing an action? Certainly, I would rather the latter. How then can we support the weak when we may not even have the resources to do so? Stop for a moment and consider Luk. 6:38 **Give, and you will receive. Your gift will return to you in full pressed down, shaken together to make room for more, running over, and poured into your lap. The amount you give will determine the amount you get back** (NLT). This is definitely an amazing scripture. Consider too the parable of the widow's mite (Mrk 12:41–44, Luke 21:1–4).

We do not have to have an abundance in order to give. Sometimes giving calls for a great sacrifice. And no, I am not in any way suggesting that we should be careless in our giving. In fact, I suggest the very opposite. Be sensitive to the leading of the Holy Spirit and allow Him to direct you in the ways you should give. Do not forget, though, that giving is a biblical principle that we should be a regular and normal part of our lives. Do not make excuses as to why you can't give. Just as certain necessities in our lives are important, we should view giving in the same light. Remember, giving is a gateway to blessings; thus, in order to keep that gateway open, we have to generously, graciously, and consistently give. 2 Cor. 9:7 sums it up nicely - Each of you should give what you have decided in your heart to give, not reluctantly or under compulsion, for God loves a cheerful giver.

Giving Of Our Best

For many, this may seem to be a clear-cut thing. A 'no-brainer' as some will say. For others, it goes without saying, or "It's the right thing to do." Yet for some, it may take some doing, a little bit of encouragement, or a lot of prodding. My church participates in an annual international Christmas giving campaign. This is an incredible opportunity to brighten the life of a child in another part of the world during Christmas.

We brought our shoeboxes home, and I explained to my then seven-year-old daughter that we were going to put things in the boxes to give away. After she got over her brief disappointment (for she thought they were to put gifts in for her - LOL), she promptly went to her room and got 2 stuffed animals and placed them in her box. I explained to her that we would buy gifts to put in them and that we cannot give away something that's old. She immediately corrected me and said that Mr. Monkey and Mrs. Bear were not old. In fact, she informed me, with some amount of seriousness too, that they were her FAVORITE and that I should follow her and give away some of my favorites. She even suggested that I put some of my makeup in my box to give away - haha. She thought that her favorites would now become the favorite of some other child unknown to her and would make them happy just like they made her happy.

At that moment, I was quite taken aback and impressed by her maturity and generosity. How many of us can truly be like this child? How many of us are willing to part with something of ours that we truly love and that is dear to our hearts? As I stated in the opening, this may be an easy feat for some, but for others it may be quite difficult or even an impossibility. If we are to think deeper about this idea, though, this is just what God has done for us. He gave Jesus, his only son, as a gift to us all so that we can be happy, whole, and free! He gave us His very best!

What precious things do we have that we can give to others? It does not have to be your favorite pair of shoes or that priceless piece of jewelry now! But it can be your best smile, perhaps your best attitude, or maybe just a word of encouragement. Your best may even come in the form of paying someone a kind compliment. Or it can be helping your spouse more around the house and being deliberately nicer to your family, even when you do not feel like it. The idea is that as you give of yourself, think not so much of what you are losing or but more so the impact that your thoughtfulness and generosity will have on the receiver. We should remind ourselves that everything shouldn't always be about us. There are so many people who would appreciate our love and generosity if we just spare a moment to offer it.

I know that life can sometimes be rough, and it can come at us fast and from different avenues all at once. But, as we try to navigate the waters, let's do what we can to help others sail a little better. Truth is, we need each other. Perhaps, like my daughter, you can bring yourself to give away something that means a lot - and that will be great.

Maybe you can even afford to sacrifice financially to bless someone, or it may just be greeting someone nicely and wishing them a good day as you pass them in the mornings.

Let's be more deliberate about being kind to others. I leave with you this beautiful quote to ponder on: IN A WORLD WHERE YOU CAN BE ANYTHING - BE KIND!

Try it and see how great you'll feel!

The Importance Of Gratitude

Gratitude is that sense of being thankful. Sometimes we may tend to reserve being grateful for the big moments! You know, for the times when we get that dream job or for the time we finally move into our own homes. But finding something to be thankful for in the smallest of things or in the most chaotic moment can be so rewarding, soul-stirring, and fulfilling. I challenge you, no matter how bad a situation may be, there is always something to express gratitude for. We may get busy at times and become taken up with all that is going on around us. It would be good, though, to take some time and think about all that you are grateful for, be it great or small. Try to develop that attitude of gratitude and see how much it will help to improve your overall life!

Oftentimes, when I sit and reflect on my life, there are so many things that I have to be grateful for. To say that I have come a mighty long way is an understatement. Certainly, I cannot remember every detail of my life up to this point, but what I can say, though, is that I am grateful for it all! I am grateful for all that I have as much as I am grateful for what I do not have. Believe me, there are some things that we most definitely do not want to have. I am also thankful for where I have been and how I have transitioned over time. Most of all, I am grateful for how much God has been with me through it all!

By no means is this the end, and because of that, I can say that I am grateful for the fact that I am not alone, as I have God with me as my guide, support, shield, and strong tower. What an assurance. Even as I write this, I am being flooded with the myriad of things that I can say THANKS for! My friends, there is beauty in every raindrop, joy scattered throughout every mountainside. Today, my prayer is that no matter what challenges you are facing, you will take your focus off them for just a while and turn it to the things that you are grateful for and just whisper or shout THANK YOU LORD! I guarantee you, it will make a grand difference. Be blessed!

Time to Reflect

SECTION VI: LIVING WITH WISDOM & GRACE

Stewardship • Gratitude • Generosity • Maturity • Godly Living

1. Biblical Financial Principles You Can Trust

1. How do I currently view money—fearfully, faithfully, or responsibly?

2. What area of my finances needs better stewardship?

3. How can I honor God with my giving, saving, and spending?

4. What mindset do I need to release concerning finances?

---

2. Find Joy in Giving

1. What emotions arise when I think about giving?

2. How can I become a more cheerful and intentional giver?

3. What has God given me—materially or spiritually—that I can share?

4. Who could be blessed by my generosity this week?

3. Giving Of Our Best

1. Am I giving God my best—or just what is convenient?

2. In what areas have I grown complacent?

3. What does giving my "best" look like in this season?

4. How can excellence become a way to honor God?

---

4. The Importance of Gratitude

1. What three things am I most grateful for today?

2. How has gratitude shifted my perspective in the past?

3. What daily habits can help me cultivate a grateful heart?

4. Who can I express gratitude to this week?

---

5. Don't Do It All Alone! DELEGATE

1. What responsibilities am I carrying that God never intended me to carry alone?

2. Why do I resist asking for help or delegating tasks?

3. Who in my life can support me more if I allow them?

4. What could delegation make possible in my life?

6. What Kind of Steward Are You?

1. What has God entrusted to me—talents, family, gifts, opportunities?

2. How well am I nurturing and managing these responsibilities?

3. Where do I need accountability to grow as a steward?

4. What small changes can improve my stewardship immediately?

Section VII:

PURPOSE, PROCESS
&
SPIRITUAL GROWTH.

PURPOSE, CALLING, DEVELOPMENT, GOD'S REFINING HAND.

"Being confident of this very thing, that He who began a good work in you will complete it."

(Phil. 1:6)

Purpose is never accidental; it is crafted by a God who knows the end from the beginning. Yet the path to purpose is often a journey: a process designed to mold, strengthen, and prepare us.

In this section, you will explore the seasons, lessons, and refining moments that shape your spiritual growth.

Here, you will discover that what may feel uncomfortable is often the very environment God uses to bring out the best in you. Trust the process; there is glory unfolding in every step.

Secret Moments with God

Sa. 91 is a popular passage that opens with the line "**He that dwelleth in the secret place of the most high shall abide under the shadow of the Almighty**". These are powerful words that, if acted upon, will yield great outcomes. Scripture also implores us to assemble with other believers (Heb. 10:25). While regular fellowship with other believers is very important for spiritual growth, spending secret moments with God is equally important. There are certain benefits to be had when we are deliberate about spending time alone with God.

In the present-day society, there can be so much 'noise'. There are multiple things to distract us from coming into personal fellowship with God. There are obligations that we must fulfil, families to take care of, deadlines to meet, bills to pay - I could go on. Despite all these, we have to be resolute and keep on pursuing secret moments with God. It is in these secret moments with God that He will, in turn, reveal His secrets to us. It's where we will receive divine downloads and deeper revelations. It's where we will receive answers and divine directives that will change the trajectory and pace of our lives. In the secret place with God is where we can gain access to both physical and spiritual healing and receive a refreshing for our souls (Psa. 23: 3).

You see, when we enter that secret place with God, we do not have to be afraid. We can be open, vulnerable, and frank with him. In fact, nothing surprises God! So, go ahead and bear your soul! Tell it like it is! Let it all out! The truth is, God already knows and has been patiently waiting for us to take it to Him in prayer. Let the praise and worship flow unhindered whenever you encounter God in secret moments. Bask in the fullness and glory of His magnificent love. As you present your petitions before Him, rest assured that He loves and cares deeply about every facet of your life and will work every detail out just perfectly.

Here's the interesting part: the secret place can be anywhere! It is not limited to a specific spot. Remember, God is omnipresent (Psa. 139: 7-10). Therefore, we can create that secret place just about anywhere we are - be it in our home, in our car, at our workstation, at our favorite outdoor space - just about anywhere! There is no need to get caught up in not being able to gain access to that particular 'spot' where we have our secret encounter with our Maker. We can create that secret place wherever we are - it is more of a state than it is a place. So, go ahead and have secret moments with God just about anywhere and anytime, for you will only be blessed by it.

Prayer - An Oasis In The Desert

An oasis is a fertile spot in a desert where water is found. Imagine going through a parched, dry, arid area. You lack water, the heat is intense, and all you can see around you is dryness, barrenness, nothing! Not a beautiful or hopeful situation, right? Your body weakens and cries out for water, for rest, for restoration. The thoughts of giving up cross your mind because you don't know just how long you will last, but you are a fighter; giving up is not an option. Slowly, you trudge on, not knowing how much further you can go. Suddenly, you see it far off on the horizon - signs of life, greenery. There is hope awaiting you, so you muster up all the strength that you can find and push on towards the awaiting oasis.

Ps. 23:3a reads He restoreth my soul. For something to be restored, it means that it was once in good condition but got worn out and then received an intervention to bring it back to its former good state. Prayer has the same effect on us. Life in general can feel like we are going through the desert. The elements sometimes batter us; the problems bombard us; the issues weigh us down, and we may feel as though we just cannot endure it. We may become physically and emotionally drained. Depression and anxiety may even creep in because things around us may seem so hopeless.

There is hope in God, and we can access restoration, redemption, and hope through praying to Him. Prayer is a direct channel between God and us. We do not need a mediator or interpreter, nor do we need permission to gain access. We can pray anywhere, anytime, and for however long we would like. Praying doesn't have to be complex; in fact, it can be quite simple. Romans 8:26 reads, "**Likewise the Spirit helps us in our weakness. For we do not know what to pray for as we ought, but the Spirit himself intercedes for us with groanings too deep for words.**" The truth is, sometimes we cannot even find words to articulate our feelings to God, and He knows this; hence, He understands, even our groanings.

When your soul feels broken and empty and in need of restoration, turn to God in prayer. When the heat and pressures of life try to overpower you, remember that you have an Advocate who you can cry out to. So, open up to Him through prayer - even in the simplest form and watch Him pour back life into you. There is restoration for you even in the desert. Your oasis awaits, so PRAY.

Persevere In Prayer

The odds may be against you more than you think you have the strength to surpass! Your physical and spiritual strength may be failing, and you may be at the point where you feel as though you cannot make it an inch farther. You have prayed, you have cried, you might even have turned to those around you for help, but there is still no ease! You still feel empty, hopeless, and lost!

This may not be the solution you wish to hear, but PERSEVERE IN PRAYER! Pray one more time! Remember, we are humans, and we may feel like enough is enough, and the burdens are just too many to carry; however, God still has you in his purview. His eyes are still watching over you! What He desires is your FAITH! Of course, He knows your circumstances are tough! Rest assured, He knows that you cry, are in mental, physical, and emotional pain, and He can and will deliver you! Just PERSEVERE IN PRAYER! Remember too that "Tears are a language that God understands", and though there is a possibility that you may weep all night, for surety, JOY SHALL come in the morning! It's not over for you! The end has not yet come!

You have more strength, tenacity, grit, and resilience embedded within you that you can even imagine. That which you face is not meant to bend or even kill you but to build and propel you. This too shall pass, just you PERSEVERE IN PRAYER! Remember too that prayer shouldn't be seen as an antidote that is taken only during difficult times, but as a daily supplement that nourishes the spirit daily and a defense from the enemy. So, PERSEVERE IN PRAYER, my friends.

Reflect on these scriptures, especially as you endure the harsh seasons of life, continue to look to God and PERSEVERE IN PRAYER!

1 Thes. 5:17 - **Pray without ceasing**

Jm. 1:6 - **But let him ask in faith, nothing wavering**.

Luk.18:1 - **Men ought always to pray, and not to faint**

Heb. 11:6 - **Without faith it is impossible to please God**

Cured In The Fire

From an early age, we learned that fire is dangerous and we should stay away from it. If we were unfortunate enough to be burned, then we would know firsthand just how unpleasant that experience is. Fire is a necessity, however, and is quite valuable. It gives warmth, provides energy for important tasks such as cooking, etc. So too, in a symbolic way, fire is needed in a believer's life because through fiery situations healing and deliverance can come.

Mal. 3:2 talks about the Refiner's fire and how he will purify the Levites and refine them like gold and silver. The analogy of gold and silver being purified is a powerful one because it gives a vivid description of the process that must be passed through in order to have our impurities removed. Quite a tough process, but an absolutely good one if we are to be free, if we are to grow, if we are to be healed - then we must go through the fire. In fact, 1 Pet. 4:12 reminds us not to think it strange concerning the fiery trial. It goes on further to say that our response to the fiery trials should be to rejoice. Strange, right? Rejoicing is the last thing on our mind when we are experiencing difficult and traumatic life circumstances.

We may ask questions such as Why did this happen to me? Why am I going through this? Or say I did nothing to deserve it. There is, however, a lesson, or even a ministry, wrapped up in your fiery situation. Having experienced the harsh situation first-hand qualifies us to be able to help others who have gone through or will go through something similar. Remember Job? He came to this conclusion, '**But he knows the way that I take; when he has tested me, I will come forth as gold**.' (Job. 23:10)

The testing period is uncomfortable, and we don't want to be there! Remember, though, that you will come out of that period cured. Being cured can be viewed in a twofold manner. Think of being cured, considering these two definitions:

- ➤ Relieve (a person or animal) of the symptoms of a disease or condition.
- ➤ Preserve (meat, fish, tobacco, or animal skin) by various methods

You see, either way, it's a win, and you'll leave the fire not just relieved but also preserved. What a blessing!

Deliverance in the situation

I came across a clip of a sermon once, and something that the preacher said caught my attention. She noted that many times when we are in a bad situation, we ask God to deliver us *from* the situation, but we should instead ask God to deliver us *in* the situation. At first, I did not get this. However, not long after it clicked.

If you are anything like me, you would rather avoid negative situations altogether. Take for example, if you work in a toxic environment where it seems like everything and everyone is against you. In such situations, the first instinct might be to remove yourself and seek another place of employment. You may begin to ask God to open doors for you so that you can get another job - this is deliverance *from* the situation. However, being delivered *in* the situation might look like God allowing you to stay in the work environment, whilst giving you the grace to cope and using you as a beacon of hope within the said work environment.

Several bible characters come to mind who are the epitome of being delivered in their situation as opposed to being delivered from it. Let's talk about Joseph. He was despised by his siblings (scripture); tossed in a pit (Gen. 37:24); sold into slavery (Gen. 37:27-28); wrongfully accused (Gen. 39:11-20); thrown into prison (Gen.39-19-20); and not remembered (Gen. 40:23). Certainly, God could have stepped in during any one of those times and delivered Joseph *from* those adverse situations, but he did not. Instead, he allowed him to go through each of them. Then, it was while Joseph was still in prison that his breakthrough came. Think about Daniel and the Hebrew boys. God could have prevented them from being thrown into the lion's den and the fiery furnace (Dan. 3:8-25; 6:16-24), but He did not. He allowed them to go through these situations and delivered them in it so that He could get the glory.

Just the same, God wants the glory from your situation; thus, he may choose not to deliver you *from* it, but deliver you *in it.* So, instead of asking God to deliver us *from* situations, understand that His **thoughts are not your thoughts, neither are His ways my ways** *(*Isa. 55: 8-9**).** While we may not be able to understand God's logic, be fine with that and learn to trust Him and simply have faith in Him. Instead of trying to abscond from every adverse situation, how about you just be **still and see the salvation of the Lord** (Ex. 14:13). Watch Him save you from that situation that you feel is about to destroy you. Remember, what the enemy intends for evil, God turns it to good (Gen 50:20).

Seasons Change

There are four natural seasons - Spring, Summer, Winter, and Autumn/Fall. In many parts of the world, each season is marked by distinct features, whilst in others, the difference is not so pronounced. Sometimes there is torrential rainfall, and at other times the land is parched and dry due to drought. The same is true with our lives - there are different seasons, and as great or as bad as they are, they change. Certainly, we welcome the thought of the bad seasons changing, but the idea of our good season changing can be frightening; however, this is a reality.

Eccles. 3 starts off by announcing that **"To everything there is a season"** and then goes on to give examples of various opposing pairs to solidify this concept. There can be great value in our lives if we were to fully embrace the reality that seasons change. During the good seasons, we should embrace them and enjoy every moment of it, but being fully mindful that there lies the grand possibility that some amount of disruption may come to this awesome season. By recognizing this possibility and proactively preparing for it, it can definitely lessen the severity of its impact. Think about it, for people who live in areas where there are harsh Winter seasons, for example, because they know this, they spend time preparing for it. As a result, winter is more tolerable for them.

Similarly, when we are experiencing a tumultuous season, we should constantly remind ourselves that too shall pass. 2 Cor. 4:17-18 talks about the **light and momentary troubles** that we will experience in this life. They are not permanent. Dark clouds don't stay forever. Stormy seas will eventually come to a calm. The drought will someday be over with a downpour of rain. So, take courage knowing that better days are ahead. Remember that **weeping *may* endure for a night, but joy comes in the morning** (Psa. 30:5). The tough season is bound to end, no doubt about that.

Every season comes with its own lessons and its own advantages. We should therefore try to make the most of each season. Be flexible; be adaptable; know how to discern the different seasons as they come and apply the necessary knowledge and wisdom that will successfully take us through them. Prayerfully ask the Lord what lessons He has for you in each season. I guarantee you that there is a valuable lesson in all seasons - the good and the bad seasons alike.

He has employed us to deploy us

So you have given your heart to the Lord; you have surrendered your life and will to Him; you are saved. Hallelujah! Now, what's next? Salvation is sweet. There is something satisfying about knowing that you have found a safe haven for your soul. In the arms of sweet deliverance - oh, what a place to be! Salvation is very personal. However, it does not stop there. God has employed us to deploy us.

Think about it, which country enlists soldiers just to have them remain always in the barracks? Doesn't sound very practical, right? So it is with disciples of Christ, while our salvation secures an eternal home with Christ, we are saved for more than that. While God can, through His divine powers, accomplish whatever He desires here in the earthly realms, He depends on us to be ambassadors in His kingdom here on earth. In Mat. 28:18-20, the great commission can be found. Here Christ implores us to -Go and make disciples of ALL nations. We are also expected to teach. Such an awesome and fulfilling task has been entrusted to us.

You see, giving our hearts to Christ is a personal, life-changing experience. No one has even given their heart to the Lord and remained the same, no one! One of the most powerful testimonies that we can ever share is that of our personal salvation story. Luk. 8:16 rightly says that **"No one, when he has lit a lamp, covers it with a**

vessel or puts *it* under a bed, but sets *it* on a lampstand, that those who enter may see the light." Why then should we be quiet about our salvation?

Certainly, our deployment will look very different. Some may end up ministering in faraway lands among people with different customs and languages from their own. Some might be deployed in official ministerial offices, such as pastoral and evangelism. Others of us might only be deployed in the community where we have lived all our lives to touch the lives of those in our locale. The point is, though, that we are all called; there is something in the vineyard of God's kingdom for all of us to do. I challenge you to rise to this call. I leave with you Col 3:23-24 **"Whatever you do, work at it with all your heart, as working for the Lord, not for human masters, since you know that you will receive an inheritance."**

The light we carry is for the world

I recently came across the song *Light* by Rotimikeys and became captivated by the opening line that states, "This light I carry is for the world. It immediately drew me to Mat. 5:16 that tells us to **"Let your light so shine before men"**. Indeed, we all have a Light within us, the light of Christ. One of the main purposes of light is to change darkness. Darkness is simply the absence of light. No matter how dark an area is, the minute that light shows up, it becomes less dark, and as more light comes into play, the darkness diminishes gradually.

We live in a world that is filled with darkness. Evil, hatred, sadness, pain, and mayhem are all around. A simple act, such as turning on the evening news, is enough to cause someone to become discouraged and hopeless. It is for these reasons that we need to shine our light. The world needs the Light that we carry. The world needs Christ, and the onus is on us to offer hope and courage to those around us.

We are the hands and feet of Christ on the earth. Certainly, He can reach whomever He wills through supernatural ways such as dreams, visions, and other forms of miraculous encounters. Nonetheless, we have a mandate, a call, a purpose! We must shine!

There are numerous ways that we can display the light of Christ on a daily basis. We can be a witness to others. One of the most powerful ways to display our Light is to live in a manner that displays the love of Christ. Another way is to testify about how Christ has changed your life. Tell of how he has transformed you. There is hope and restoration in your testimony, so use this as a tool to light the path for others. There is enough cruelty around us, and so we are tasked to show love and tenderness to those with whom we come in contact. Instead of being harsh like everyone else, we can choose to be gentle. Remember, **No man, when he hath lighted a candle, putteth it in a secret place, neither under a bushel, but on a candlestick, that they which come in may see the light. (Matt. 5:16)**

You are special and filled with purpose! You do not exist by sheer coincidence. You belong to Christ, and as such, you are filled with His light. This Light is life-altering, and others are depending on you to shine brightly and be the guide to get them out of dark tunnels. So, ask the Lord to show you ways to display His light daily for the benefit of others. Also, partner with other Light-carriers to flood the world with the light of Christ because it is needed. Shine on, Light-carrier!

Living Purposefully

What is my WHY? What is my purpose? Why am I here? Why was I created? We might contemplate such questions from time to time. Some people have successfully identified and are actively living out their purpose, while others have yet to discover theirs. Your purpose is your why on earth. It's the reason you are here, and it is my firm belief that until we identify and embrace our purpose, we will not feel fulfilled and totally satisfied. Living outside of our life's true purpose is dull and might even feel meaningless. It therefore behooves us to prayerfully seek the Lord and ask Him to reveal to us what our purpose is.

Do not fall into the trap that you are too insignificant to have any purpose at all. You might even ask yourself, 'What use can God really have for me to do?' We may even try to find excuses to comfort ourselves and feed ourselves lies such as 'I do not have the necessary resources', 'I am not qualified', 'I am sure that there is someone better than me for this task', etc. Again, the simple truth is that you were created for a purpose. In fact, your purpose existed even before you did, ask Jeremiah (Jer. 1:5). Scripture also clearly states that **those whom He foreknew, He also predestined** (Rom. 8:29).

Another pitfall to avoid as we endeavor to live purposefully is busyness without a true cause. We should not mistake a busy life for a purposeful life. The two are not the same, and while living purposefully might lead to busyness, busyness does not automatically equate to operating in our purpose. The sooner we know and understand the difference, the better it will be for us. We can be busy doing the wrong things. Let's not be busy doing things that God did not call us to do, whilst we neglect the very purpose that He is trying to lead us to.

Obedience is an integral component if we are to fulfill our life's purpose. We first have to be obedient to God's will for us and to accept whatever purpose He lays in our charge. He knows far more than we can ever know, so the onus is on us to simply trust Him. After all, His will is perfect (Rom. 12:2). So, find your why and walk boldly and unapologetically in it.

YOLO - So make it count!

Life is so precious, so very wonderful, but also very fragile. We do not know how long we are here for. We have no idea what the next minute will bring. One minute we might be up and about, and everything is 'normal', then, in the next instant, catastrophe strikes and everything changes for the worse. We may be healthy and strong one day and then no longer after we begin struggling with a health issue. These realities are sobering and can even be frightening, but it's reality. Life is unpredictable, and the sooner we understand this truth, the better it is for us.

The term YOLO - You Only Live Once - is one that is often thrown around lightly. Sadly, it is even used as an excuse to live in a reckless manner. It should, however, serve as a constant reminder that indeed we only live once, and the life choices that we make now determine both the quality of life here on earth in the future and how we will spend eternity. Since we only live once then it makes sense to seek to make the most of this one opportunity. Certainly, it is debatable about what making the most of our lives might look like. One way to measure this is to live in accordance with the ordinances and will of God.

God has given us His holy scriptures that we can use as a guide as we navigate life. Living our best life definitely involves surrendering our all to Christ - our thoughts, plans, desires - *everything*. We shouldn't invite God into some areas of our lives and hold on to the reins in other areas. We have to give him everything - our careers, our love interests, our finances, our gifts and talents - all of it. Surrender every facet of your life to Christ and watch Him shape out your best life. Surrendering to Christ begins with salvation - accepting Christ as Lord, believing that Jesus died for our sins, and confessing our sins. A word of caution, though, salvation alone doesn't guarantee that we will have a good life. There has to be obedience, faith, and work! After all, **faith without works is dead** (Jas. 2:20)

Do not let the world fool you into believing that the sins and pleasures of this world are what will guarantee that you have a good life. Not so! A good life is one that is Christ-centered, where the divine will of God for our lives is allowed to take shape. A good life is one that is lived with passion and dedication to the things that are pleasing to God. So, each and every day, let it be at the forefront of your mind that YOLO. How will you use this one chance?

Time to Reflect

SECTION VII: PURPOSE, PROCESS & SPIRITUAL GROWTH

Calling • Seasons • Refinement • God's Plan • Spiritual Maturity

1. Prayer – An Oasis in the Desert

1. What role does prayer play in my everyday life?

2. When has prayer felt like an oasis for me?

3. What area of my life needs more intentional prayer?

4. How can I deepen my intimacy with God through prayer?

---

2. Persevere in Prayer

1. What prayer request have I abandoned out of discouragement?

2. How can I develop consistency and endurance in prayer?

3. What does perseverance in prayer mean to me personally?

4. Where have I already seen God respond to persistent prayer?

3. Cured in the Fire

1. What difficult situation has refined me the most?

2. What qualities has God developed in me through trials?

3. How has the "fire" shaped my character?

4. How can I see adversity as preparation instead of punishment?

---

4. Deliverance in the Situation

1. What situation do I need deliverance from right now?

2. How has God delivered me in the past?

3. What steps of obedience or faith do I sense God prompting me to take?

4. How can I remain hopeful while waiting for a breakthrough?

---

5. He Has Employed Us to Deploy Us

1. What gifts or skills has God placed in me for service?

2. How am I using those gifts for His kingdom?

3. What opportunity or assignment might God be preparing me for?

4. How can I remain faithful in the "employment" phase as God prepares to deploy me?

6. The Light We Carry Is for the World

1. Where have I been hiding my light—intentionally or unintentionally?

2. Who needs the light, encouragement, or wisdom that God has placed within me?

3. How can I shine more boldly without fear of judgment?

4. What does it look like to be a light in my home, workplace, or community?

7. Seasons Change

1. What old season am I still clinging to that God is asking me to release?

2. What new season might God be ushering me into?

3. How can I embrace change with grace instead of fear?

4. What beauty can I identify in the season I'm currently experiencing?

8. Learn From the Journey: The Outcome Has Already Been Established

1. What lessons has my journey taught me that I didn't appreciate at the time?

2. How does knowing that God has already established the outcome change my perspective?

3. What part of the journey am I currently struggling with?

4. How can I focus more on growth than on the destination?

---

9. God's Blueprint for YOU

1. What unique part of God's blueprint have I already discovered?

2. Where do I struggle to trust God's design for my life?

3. What steps can I take to align more closely with His blueprint?

4. How does God's plan differ from my own expectations?

10. Comfort Zone, the Enemy of Growth

1. Which comfort zone am I currently stuck in?

2. What growth opportunity am I avoiding because it feels uncomfortable?

3. What would obedience look like if I stepped out in faith?

4. Who would benefit from my willingness to grow?

11. Living Purposefully

1. What does living on purpose mean to me?

2. What daily habits help keep me aligned with my purpose?

3. What distractions pull me away from intentional living?

4. Who or what inspires me to live with purpose?

12. YOLO – So Make It Count!

1. If I only had one year to make an impact, what would I focus on?

2. What decisions would I make differently if I truly embraced the value of time?

3. What dream or assignment have I delayed that God wants me to pursue now?

4. How can I live each day more fully and spiritually aware?

Closing

In January 2013, while at a church convention, I received a prophetic word. It was simple yet profound – God says to WRITE! This instruction from God never left my spirit. For years, I reflected on what to write. Although I knew that I had the skills and ability to write but I did not have the least idea as to where to begin. I was at a loss.

It wasn't until the very end of 2019, when I was going through a very rough patch in life, that I took the first step and started a blog.

At first, there was some amount of consistency where I would write a blog entry every now and then. Then I began to lose interest and momentum. Then, sometime in 2024, the Lord revealed to me the venue where He wanted me to host my book launch. A BOOK LAUNCH? Really? I at least need to have a book in order to have a launch, right? Not long after, someone shared with me a dream that he had of me with a pen (or a pencil – I don't quite remember). Clearly, this was the Lord reminding me that I had an unfinished task that He wanted me to get back to.

It was a little bit daunting, to be honest. I began to give myself deadlines, only not to meet them. At points, I felt as though I just would not be able to finish. Doubt crept in. Busyness presented itself. I mustered up all the determination that I could and pushed ahead.

Today, it is surreal to think that I have FINISHED my first book, and for that I can only praise God!

If, like me, God has tasked you with an assignment, and it seems as if you just cannot accomplish it. I want to encourage you that you can. You are equipped for this task, and with persistence, you can complete it.

From my own experience and from my encounter with women of different ages and from diverse cultures, I am well aware of the many obstacles that women face. What I am also aware of, too, is the unmatched strength that lies within a woman who is focused and determined to WIN. A woman who is fueled by faith in God is unstoppable – you are that woman!

I pray that as you read VIALS OF WISDOM FOR THE WINNING WOMAN that you have found strength, wisdom, and clarity on these pages.

My final word to you, WINNER, is -

Walk confidently, fully grounded in God's Word, Wisdom, and Purpose

Please share how these vials have blessed you by sending me an email at womenofpowerimprovingnicely@gmail.com.

Consider blessing someone with a copy of this book too.

You can even consider deliberately placing a copy in a public, and ask God to lead the right reader to it.

Please, leave a review on Amazon if you purchased this book there.

You can also find me on YouTube by looking up Women of Power Improving Nicely or scanning the QR Code below.

Closing Prayer

Gracious God,

Again, I thank you for giving me wisdom and insights to write this book.

Father, I present every individual who has read it – please bless them in every area of their lives. Lord, I ask that you continually work on every heart and bring healing, deliverance, and victory into the lives of your people. I pray that they will find comfort knowing that you care deeply about them and know that there is no situation that is too difficult for you to fix. Where salvation and total surrender to Your will are needed – I ask that you allow these to happen.

Abba, help every reader to embrace the truth that You desire for them to WIN and through a deeper relationship with You – they can live a triumphant and fruitful life.

I ask these in the name of Your Son – Jesus Christ.

Benediction

The Lord bless you

and keep you;

the Lord make his face shine on you

and be gracious to you;

the Lord turn his face toward you

and give you peace.

(Numb. 6:24-26)

Appendix

Further Reflection Questions

PART I: THE HEART OF A WINNING WOMAN & SPIRITUAL MATURITY

Identity • Inner Healing • Emotional Courage •

Maturity in Christ

1. What beliefs about myself align with God's truth, and which ones do I need to release?

2. Where in my life is God inviting me to mature emotionally or spiritually?

3. How have past hurts shaped me, and what healing is God offering to me now? How readily am I receiving this healing?

4. What would my life look like if I truly lived as a "winning woman"?

5. What emotions or memories do I need to surrender in order to grow?

6. Which strengths has God placed in me that I haven't fully embraced or shied away from?

7. What step can I take today toward becoming the woman God sees in me?

✦ PART II: RELATIONSHIPS, LOVE & COMMUNITY

Friendships • Love • Boundaries • Connection • Support Systems

1. Who/What in my life consistently draws me closer to God, and who/what pulls me away from Him?

2. What boundaries do I need to honor to protect my emotional and spiritual health?

3. How can I strengthen meaningful relationships while still valuing healthy solitude so that I can grow deeper in my relationship with Christ?

4. What relationships require forgiveness, restoration, or release?

5. How do I experience God's love through the people He has placed in my life?

6. Am I a source of encouragement and love to the community around me? If not, how can I be more deliberate about this?

7. How can I cultivate and sustain deeper, Christ-centered friendships?

✦ PART III: EMOTIONAL & MENTAL WELL-BEING

Thought Life • Emotional Balance • Mental Clarity • Inner Peace

1. What thoughts most frequently consume my mind, and do they align with God's Word?

2. What situations tend to trigger emotional overwhelm in me?

3. How do I currently respond to stress, and how can I respond in a more Christlike manner?

4. What emotions have I minimized or buried that God is calling me to confront and expel?

5. What do I need to release mentally in order to experience God's peace?

6. How can I practice gentleness, kindness, and patience with myself?

7. What does emotional and mental wellness look like for me in this season and beyond?

8. What practical steps can I take towards achieving wholeness?

✨ PART IV: RISING IN STRENGTH & PURPOSE

Confidence • Action • Courage • Resilience • Bold Steps of Faith

1. What area of my life is God calling me to rise higher in right now?

2. What fears or doubts do I need to confront so that I can move forward?

3. Where is God nudging me to take bold, courageous action?

4. How have challenges shaped me into a stronger version of myself?

5. What distractions must I eliminate to stay focused on my purpose?

6. What would my life look like if I fully walked in my God-given strength and calling?

7. How can I show up as the "Proverbs 31" version of myself each day?

7. ✦ PART V: TRUST, DISCIPLINE & DIVINE ALIGNMENT

Faith • Surrender • Waiting • Obedience • Listening for God's Voice

1. What area of my life is God inviting me to surrender FULLY?

2. How do I typically respond to seasons of waiting, and how can I trust God more deeply?

3. When was the last time I felt God's silence? What did I learn from it?

4. What promises from God do I need to anchor myself in right now?

5. What spiritual disciplines (prayer, fasting, study) do I need to strengthen?

6. How can I align my daily choices more closely with God's will for my life?

7. Where have I seen God's faithfulness even when I didn't understand His timing?

✦ PART VI: LIVING WITH WISDOM & GRACE

Stewardship • Generosity • Gratitude • Humility • Godly

Living

1. How am I stewarding the resources, gifts, and opportunities God has given me?

2. What areas of my life need more wisdom and intentionality?

3. How can I cultivate a deeper habit of gratitude each day?

4. In what ways can I live more generously: with my time, talent, and compassion?

5. Where am I relying on my own strength instead of God's guidance?

6. What responsibilities do I need to delegate for better balance or growth?

7. How can I demonstrate grace toward others (and myself) more consistently?

✦ PART VII: PURPOSE, PROCESS & SPIRITUAL GROWTH

Calling • Refinement • Seasons • Assignment • Maturing in Your Walk with God

1. What season am I currently in: planting, waiting, pruning, or harvesting?

2. What is God calling my attention to during this season?

3. What has God been teaching me through recent challenges?

4. What part of my calling have I embraced, and what part have I avoided?

5. How can I better align my daily actions with my God-given purpose?

6. What spiritual habits or attitudes must I develop to grow further?

7. What legacy do I want my life to reflect as God continues to refine me?

Devotional Prompts

PART I: THE HEART OF A WINNING WOMAN & SPIRITUAL MATURITY

Identity • Forgiveness • Healing • Emotional Courage

1. Ask God: *"Where in my heart do You desire to heal me?"*

2. Write a declaration about who God says you are.

3. Pray for strength to forgive where needed.

4. Journal: What "old version" of me is God calling me to shed?

5. Spend 3 minutes thanking God for the strengths He placed in you.

PART II: RELATIONSHIPS, LOVE & COMMUNITY

Friendship • Love • Boundaries • Support

1. Ask the Holy Spirit: *"Who in my life needs my love today?"*

2. Pray over your closest relationships by name.

3. Journal the relationships that bring you closer to God.

4. Spend time alone and reflect: *What is God saying in the quiet?*

5. Write a prayer of gratitude for people who have supported you.

PART III: EMOTIONAL & MENTAL WELL-BEING

Thought Life • Peace • Stability • Emotional Balance

1. Identify one recurring thought—and replace it with a Scripture.

2. Pray: *"Lord, renew my mind today."*

3. Journal how God has given you peace before.

4. Take 5 deep breaths and repeat: "God is in control."

5. Ask God: *"What do I need to rest from emotionally?"*

PART IV: RISING IN STRENGTH & PURPOSE

Courage • Action • Overcoming • Confidence

1. Journal a moment God strengthened you in the past.

2. Pray for boldness to take one difficult step.

3. Ask God: *"What task have You assigned to me?"*

4. Declare: "I am strong in the Lord and in His mighty power."

5. Write down the distraction you need to release this week.

PART V: TRUST, DISCIPLINE & DIVINE ALIGNMENT

Faith • Waiting • Surrender • Obedience

1. Pray: *"Lord, align my desires with Yours."*

2. Ask God: *"What area of my life do I need to surrender?"*

3. Journal about a time God came through unexpectedly.

4. Meditate on a promise Scripture for 5 minutes.

5. Write a prayer for patience in your current season.

PART VI: LIVING WITH WISDOM & GRACE

Stewardship • Gratitude • Balance • Generosity

1. Ask God: *"What have You entrusted to me?"*

2. Journal how you can better steward time, gifts, or resources.

3. Write a gratitude prayer.

4. Choose one way to give generously this week.

5. Pray for wisdom in one specific decision.

PART VII: PURPOSE, PROCESS & SPIRITUAL GROWTH

Calling • Seasons • Refinement • God's Blueprint

1. Ask God: *"What season am I in?"*

2. Journal how God has been shaping your character.

3. Pray for clarity concerning your purpose.

4. Write down the lesson God is teaching you right now.

5. Declare: "God is guiding my steps."

Scripture by Theme Index

FAITH

- Matthew 19:26 — With God all things are possible

- Mark 10:27 — Nothing is impossible with God

- Luke 1:37 — Nothing is impossible with God

- Luke 18:27 — God can do what humans cannot

- Romans 8:28 — God works all things for our good

- Romans 8:37 — More than conquerors

- Romans 12:19 — Vengeance belongs to God

- 2 Corinthians 5:17 — New creation in Christ

- 2 Corinthians 12:9 — His grace is sufficient

- Ephesians 3:20 — Exceedingly abundantly above all

- Hebrews 11:6 — Without faith it is impossible to please God

- James 1:6 — Ask in faith, not wavering

- James 2:26 — Faith without works is dead

- 1 Peter 4:12 — Fiery trials are not strange

- 1 John 4:4 — Greater is He that is in you

STRENGTH & ENCOURAGEMENT

- Deuteronomy 32:35 — Vengeance is the Lord's

- Psalm 27:13 — Seeing the goodness of the Lord

- Psalm 30:5 — Weeping may endure for a night, joy comes in the morning

- Psalm 46:1 — God is our refuge and strength

- Isaiah 55:8–9 — God's ways and thoughts are higher

- Jeremiah 29:11 — Plans to prosper us and give hope

- Matthew 11:29–30 — His yoke is easy and burden light

- Mark 4:35–41 — Jesus calms the storm

- 1 Corinthians 10:13 — God provides a way of escape

- Hebrews 13:5 — God will never leave nor forsake

- Job 23:10 — Coming forth as gold after testing

FORGIVENESS & LETTING GO

- Matthew 5:23–24 — Reconcile before offering your gift

- Matthew 18:21–22 — Forgive seventy times seven

- Matthew 18:23–35 — Parable of the unmerciful servant

- Romans 13:8 — Owe no man anything except love

- 2 Corinthians 5:17 — Old things passed away, all things made new

- Hebrews 12:14 — Live peaceably with all

- 1 Peter 4:10 — Stewards of God's grace (linked to forgiveness and service)

PURPOSE & CALLING

- Genesis 12 — Abraham called to step out in faith

- Jeremiah 29:11 — Hope and a future

- Proverbs 3:5 — Trust in the Lord with all your heart

- Proverbs 4:7 — Wisdom is the principal thing

- Matthew 25:14–30 — Parable of the talents (purpose, stewardship)

- Luke 19:11–17 — Faithful stewardship rewarded

- Romans 8:28 — Called according to His purpose

- 1 Corinthians 2:9 — What God has prepared for those who love Him

- Ephesians 4:6 — God above all and in all

- 1 Peter 4:10 — Use your gifts to serve others

TRIALS, SUFFERING & DELIVERANCE

- Job 14:1 — Life is full of trouble

- Job 23:10 — Testing produces refinement

- Daniel 3:8–25 — Fiery furnace

- Daniel 6:16–24 — Lion's den

- Malachi 3:2 — Refiner's fire

- Matthew 11:29–30 — Rest for the weary

- Luke 7:11–17 — Widow of Nain

- John 11 — Lazarus raised

- Romans 8:26 — Spirit intercedes in weakness

- 2 Corinthians 12:9 — Strength made perfect in weakness

- 1 Peter 4:12 — Fiery trials

HOPE & PERSEVERANCE

- Psalm 27:13 — Believing to see God's goodness

- Psalm 30:5 — Joy comes in the morning

- Ecclesiastes 10:19 — Money answers all things (used in context of practical wisdom)

- Matthew 11:29–30 — Rest for your soul

- Luke 8:43–48 — Woman with the issue of blood

- Romans 8:28 — All things work together

- 1 Thessalonians 5:17 — Pray without ceasing

- Hebrews 11:6 — Faith pleases God

PRAYER

- 1 Thessalonians 5:17 — Pray without ceasing

- Luke 18:1 — Always pray, don't faint

- Romans 8:26 — Spirit intercedes

- Hebrews 11:6 — Faith needed in prayer

- Matthew 11:29–30 — Come to Christ for rest

- James 1:6 — Ask in faith

- James 2:26 — Faith + works

STEWARDSHIP & WISE LIVING

- Proverbs 4:7 — Get wisdom

- Matthew 25:14–30 — Parable of the Talents

- Luke 19:11–17 — Stewardship and reward

- 1 Peter 4:10 — Stewardship of gifts

- Malachi 3:10–11 — Tithing and God's promise

- Ecclesiastes 10:19 — Practical financial wisdom

OVERCOMING FEAR & WORRY

- Isaiah 55:8-9 — God's ways higher

- Psalm 46:1 — God is our refuge

- Mark 4:35-41 — Jesus calms the storm

- Luke 1:37 — Nothing impossible with God

- 2 Corinthians 12:9 — Strength in weakness

- Hebrews 13:5 — God will never leave you

IDENTITY IN CHRIST

- 2 Corinthians 5:17 — New creation

- Romans 8:37 — More than conquerors

- 1 John 4:4 — Greater is He that is in you

- Jeremiah 29:11 — God's plan for your life

- Ephesians 3:20 — God's ability beyond your imagination

www.ingramcontent.com/pod-product-compliance
Lightning Source LLC
Chambersburg PA
CBHW061253120726
48001CB00001B/282